W9-AWL-230

Property Of -Anshe Emunah
Liberty Jewish Center
7000 Rockland Hill Dr.
Baltimore, MD 21209
410-653-7485

Please Do Not Remove

ROSH HASHANAH YOM KIPPUR

SURVIVAL KIT

Newly Revised & Expanded

Apisdorf understands the heartbeat of our generation with incomparable clarity; he knows where it hurts and what to do about it.

Rabbi Michel and Rebbetzin Feige Twerski - Milwaukee

The Survival Kit transforms what can be an uninspiring experience into a truly exhilarating one.

Rabbi Yaacov Weinberg - Ner Israel Rabbinical College

ROSH HASHANAH YOM KIPPUR

SURVIVAL KIT

Newly Revised & Expanded

Shimon Apisdorf

LEVIATHAN PRESS

BOOKS THAT MAKE A DIFFERENCE

Rosh Hashanah Yom Kippur Survival Kit
Newly Revised and Expanded
by Shimon Apisdorf

Copyright © 1997 Shimon Apisdorf

Leviathan Press
2505 Summerson Road
Baltimore, Maryland 21209
(410) 653-0300

Notice of Rights
All rights reserved. No part of this book may be reproduced or utilized in any form or by any means, electronic or mechanical, including photocopying, recording or by any information storage and retrieval system, without written permission from the publisher. Reviewers may quote brief passages.

Library of Congress Catalog Number: 92-81823

ISBN 1-881927-14-8

Printed in the United States of America
First edition 1992
Cover illustration by Julius Ciss (416) 784-1416
Cover and jacket design by Staiman Design
First edition jacket design by Select Design
Page layout by Fisherman Sam
Photography (the forest, the trees, author) by Miriam Apisdorf
Technical consultants: E.R./D.L./Y.B.Z.
Editorial services by Sharon Goldinger/PeopleSpeak

Distributed to the trade by NBN (800) 462-6420

All books from Leviathan Press are available at bulk order discounts for educational, promotional and fundraising purposes. For information call (800) 538-4284.

Other books by Shimon Apisdorf

Passover Survival Kit
The Survival Kit Family Haggadah
The One Hour Purim Primer: Everything a family needs to understand, celebrate and enjoy Purim.
The Death Of Cupid: Reclaiming the wisdom of love, dating, romance and marriage. By Nachum Braverman and Shimon Apisdorf
Chanukah: Eight Nights of Light, Eight Gifts for the Soul (1997)

More praise . . .

The Death of Cupid is an insightful guide to discovering the beautifully deep potential of marriage.
John Gray, Ph.D., Men Are From Mars, Women Are From Venus

The relevance of the Passover Seder comes to life with this excellent, well written guide.

Detroit Jewish News

This exciting spiritual approach to taking the old and making it new has inspired me to reexplore my Jewish values.
Deena Kranitz, JCC Young Adult Program Coordinator

Another ground-breaking book from Shimon Apisdorf. The Passover Survival Kit will undoubtedly transform Passover for all who study this remarkable manual.
Rabbi Ephraim Z. Buchwald, National Jewish Outreach Program

Response was great. I wish I could get this into the hands of every Jewish college student across the country.

Sarah Rosenthal, Director of Campus Youth Services,
Bergen County Jewish Federation

For the first time in my life I realized that Judaism could actually be relevant.
Todd J. Appelbaum, Columbus Jewish Federation Board of Trustees

... for the surface of Moses' face shone...

Dedicated to the memory of
Manfred E. Hart

who, like Moses, in a humble, passionate
way, abidingly brightened this world and all
those whom he touched.

ACKNOWLEDGEMENTS

Donna Cohen, Mark Barbour, Blair Axel, David Baum, Aron Blackman, Rick Cohen, Helen and Joe Berman, George Rohr, Oscar Rosenberg, Kim McGarvey, Sharon Green, the Baker family, Aron Hoch, Shalom Schwartz, Mitch Mandel, Irving Stone, Shaya Pister, Shlomo Gogek and family, Shimon Weiner, Baruch Rabinowitz, Rabbi Mordechai and Chaya Blumenfeld, Earl & Sari Gorman, William Schottenstein, The Shores, The Jacobs, Rabbi Michel Twerski, Rabbi Shalom Shapiro, Rav Gil, Frank Nutis, Rabbi Alan G. Ciner, Rabbi Hirsh M. Chinn, Eric Schram, Wendy Walls, Jake Koval, Michael Monson, Rick Magder, Harvey and Sheila Hecker, Yaakov and Lori Palatnik, Avraham Leibowitz, Rabbi Menachem Goldberger, Mike Berenstein, Dov Friedberg, Barry and Rita and the kids, Yehudis Silverstein, Mrs. Pauline Eisenmann, Joseph Frasco, Yitzchak Greenman, Mitchel Shore, Killer, Zale Newman and Pal.

APPRECIATION

Ann Apisdorf, sister, friend and chavrusa. Asher Resnick, a friend. Michael (you're all heart) Hart. Rebbetzin Esther Jungreis. Yossi and Judy Abrams, one in a million. Yechezkal Mordechai, a teacher. Reuven. Goldie Lurie. Russell ("the Saver") Simmons, a mensch personified. Harry Apisdorf, what a brother is supposed to be. Josh Greenberg. Sam Glaser, music for the soul. Arthur Rosenthal. Aish HaTorah, my teachers and friends. Rabbi Noah Weinberg, Rosh Hayeshiva and source of inspiration.

SPECIAL THANKS

My parents, David and Bernice Apisdorf, who possess the courage to allow their children to chart their own course all the while building a close and loving family. Welcome back to Shaker Hts.

Mr. and Mrs. Robert and Charlotte Rothenburg, whose love and kindness know no bounds.

Esther Rivka, Ditzah Leah and Yitzchak Ben Zion. It is a privilege to have such children.

My wife, my blessing, my source of goodness. Miriam. A woman of valor whose love, dedication and hands-on involvement have shaped every page of this book as she does every day of our life together. Miriam, my hero.

Hakadosh Baruch Hu, source of all blessing.

CONTENTS

ROSH HASHANAH: THE FOREST

Yom Kippur: THE TREES

INTRODUCTION

— I —

So Much to Do, So Little Time

A few years ago a Canadian radio station aired a documentary series that looked at early twentieth century inventions touted as products that would "change your life." There is no doubt that the last one hundred years have been replete with products and inventions that have indeed altered the way we live. It's hard to imagine what life would be like without disposable plastic wraps, containers and bottles—can you believe that milk once came in a glass bottle? From telephones to fax machines and then to e-mail—who knows what's next? Maybe "Beam me up, Scotty" is just around the corner.

There is one part of that documentary that still stays with me: It's the piece about early advertisements for the first sewing machines. It seems that the assumption underlying the content and tone of those ads was, *what will women do with all the free time they will now have on their hands*? It was clear that the sewing machine would usher in an era of leisure totally unprecedented in the history of mankind.

The irony, of course, is that with the plethora of devices and services designed to save us time and increase our efficiency, we seem to have less time and be more harried than ever before. It's a catch-22, of sorts. The more time we have, the more we can do, and the more we can do, the more time we need. Hence, we try to fill every hour saved by our PC with two hours of other work or fun (mostly work), thus pushing us to discover ways to create another additional hour of time to accommodate the increased load. This deadly cycle soon spawns a new generation of time-saving inventions, which are again followed by more activities to fill the new empty spaces. The result is that what once took a week now takes a day and what once took a month or more, is now only a week's work.

Are you still puzzled at the fact that we are a society running on empty? We are forever burning ourselves out trying to manage our time and compress many years worth of activities into just one twelve-month slot. Eventually, something has to give.

Judaism: Caught in the Squeeze

There exists today an intense competition over who and what will fill the ever-shrinking discretionary time in our schedules. Where once Judaism was printed in strong, bold letters across our calendars, today it is lucky to get "penciled in" for even a few days in the entire year.

If Judaism were a corporation, I would assert that it has done a miserable job of marketing itself to the sophisticated, discerning consumer of the last half of the twentieth century. It is my contention, however, that the issue is one of marketing and packaging, not one of product quality. This doesn't mean that Judaism should suddenly take to the airwaves with a slick Madison Avenue ad campaign (although it's a thought), but rather that we should look at the medium through which the message of Judaism has been communicated these last several decades and see if we can't understand the problems and offer a solution.

Just Do It and Don't Ask Questions

The dominant medium for communicating Judaism to this generation has been the synagogue or community Hebrew schools. Whatever Jewish education most Jews possess today came from those after-school or Sunday morning classes that we all swore we would never subject our children to. Another medium was our parents or grandparents. While no one can dispute that their hearts were deeply rooted in the right place, the fact remains that even the deepest of sentiments in no way readied them for the task of articulating Jewish values in a relevant and cogent manner. More often than not, their fallback position was, "We do it because we're Jewish and that's just the way it is." And for better or worse, such an argument no longer carries the weight it once did.

We find ourselves in a bewildering world. We want to make sense of what we see around us and to ask: What is the nature of the universe? Where is our place in it and where did it and we come from? Why is it the way it is? Up to now, most scientists have been too occupied with the development of new theories that describe what *the universe is to ask the question* why.

Stephen W. Hawking, <u>A Brief History Of Time</u>

The same, I believe, can be said about Judaism today. As educated adults who happen to be Jewish, we tend to look at our religious heritage and find it to be rather bewildering. We would like to make sense of it, to find for ourselves a place within it, but we just aren't sure what to make of the whole thing.

To a degree, the quandary of Jewish identity also stems from a prominent focus on the what and how of Jewish life at the expense of the why. A great problem is that Jewish education has stressed the mechanics of Judaism (the what and the how) and has neglected the reasons, meaning and spiritual ideas behind Jewish practice (the why). In a world where people carefully consider which activities will fill their time, you had better give them a darn good reason for choosing High Holiday services over the World Series, or quite frankly, you don't stand a chance! Of course, there is always good old-fashioned Jewish guilt. But it would be tragic if the Jewish people; the people who gave the world monotheism and the universal dream of, *Nation shall not lift up sword against nation*, were left with nothing to appeal to other than the specter of callously bruising the tender feelings of an aging parent or grandparent. Surely there is something that can sustain us other than guilt.

The Why of Being Jewish

The *Rosh Hashanah Yom Kippur Survival Kit* is just the tip of an iceberg. Its purpose is to demonstrate that Judaism has nothing to be ashamed of when it comes to the superior quality of its intellectual and spiritual content. The Survival Kit assumes that if people were to possess a mature understanding of what Judaism has to say to our lives today, then it would easily hold its own in the fiercely competitive environment in which we live.

As I alluded to earlier, every aspect of Jewish life consists of three primary components. These are *what*, *how* and *why*. Let's take Passover as an example. What do you do on Passover? You make a seder. How do you make a seder? You get a box or two of matzo, some wine, a few Maxwell House haggadahs; you *shlepp* your family to the table; and presto, a seder! Then comes the issue of why. Why do we do all these things at seder? Why four cups of wine and not five? Why do we recline and so on?

Isn't it obvious that if we never meaningfully address the question of *why*, then eventually our Judaism will become a hollow sentimental ritual at best, a dreary burden at worst? In Jewish law it is considered torture to have someone perform a purposeless task. To carry out a mindless function with no comprehension of the purpose it fulfills is fine if you are dealing with automatons. For Jews, as for all people, it is ultimately debasing and inspires either total lethargy or violent revolution. The Jewish community today is confronted with both of these responses on a massive scale.

The *Rosh Hashanah Yom Kippur Survival Kit* is a partial attempt to address the issue of why, within the context of the High Holiday services. According to the most recent statistics, the majority of Jews today no longer have any synagogue affiliation whatsoever. In fact, so many young Jewish parents are disillusioned with Judaism that over half-a-million Jewish children are being raised with either no religion or with a religion other than Judaism. I would be surprised if more than 40 percent of Jews in America attend Rosh Hashanah and Yom Kippur services anymore. I would be even more surprised if more than 20 percent of those who do attend don't start looking for the exit shortly after their arrival. How can a day in synagogue possibly be meaningful or inspiring if you don't understand the meaning behind the prayers you are reciting or the concepts upon which the holiday is based?

This book has been written for three types of people. Firstly, it is for people who have given-up on formalized Judaism and who are not planning to attend synagogue this year. If this is you, then I want to make the following promise: This book will give you a radically different understanding of Rosh Hashanah, Yom Kippur and perhaps your entire Jewish identity. Read this book—I dare you—and you will find that there just might be a side to Judaism, and even to synagogue, that you can learn to enjoy and look forward to.

Secondly, if you are planning to attend services but are dreading the experience, then again, this book has been written for you. What's more, I would suggest you read it twice. Once during the weeks before Rosh Hashanah and again during the services themselves.

Lastly, if you are among those who already have some sense of the meaning of these holidays, then I think that you—perhaps more than anyone else—will find the Survival Kit to be a worthwhile intellectual and spiritual supplement to your experience in synagogue this year.

Wishing you a *Shana Tova*, a sweet new year.

Shimon Apisdorf

PROLOGUE:

WHAT'S A HOLIDAY?

—2—

Two Views of Time

C lassically, there are two models for viewing time: one linear and one cyclical. The linear view imagines time to be an infinitely long line with three component parts—past, present, and future. Today we stand in the present and if we but peer over our shoulder we will behold a long line of time stretching back deeper and deeper into the murky realm of the past. The future is simply the continuation of this same line waiting to progress endlessly ahead of us.

The cyclical notion of time conjures up a different image. In this model we keep going around and around in circles forever wearing a deeper rut in the same track. With specific regard to Jewish holidays, our concept of time more resembles the cyclical view—though not in its strictest sense—than the linear.

Holidays as Seasons

If you live in a climate that exhibits few significant seasonal changes, then you are missing out on one of life's most delightful experiences. There is nothing more enchanting than the buds of springtime working their magic to restore the trees to life, the first morning when you open your window and hear birds singing, the variegated leaves of autumn, or a silent snowfall.

In a society that moves from home to car to office and back again—each with its own background music—we barely feel the impact of the shifts in seasons. The pace is too fast. The music too loud. The loss, well, incalculable.

If, however, you make the effort to take an occasional walk and feel the moods of the seasons then, your life is so much the richer. But beyond the sheer beauty you also know that each season has a distinct feel. A resonance that your psyche responds to. There is something special in the air in springtime. And yes, in the fall it's there too—all together different, but no less enchanting.

So it is with the holidays. More than once the annual cycle of the Jewish year has been dubbed "seasons of the soul." Each spring we pack away our layers of sweaters and dust the winter's dormancy off our bicycle seats. We're free again. Just like we were last spring, only not quite.

Each year Passover comes. We pack away the bread products and dust off those grape juice–stained *haggadahs*. In Hebrew, Passover is labeled *Z'man Heruteynu*—the time of our freedom. We're free again. Just like we were last Passover, only not quite.

Seasons as Opportunities

Every holiday has its own personality, its own feel. There is a singular opportunity for personal growth that exists within the observance of each holiday that is present at no other time during the year.

Passover is called *the time of our freedom* because at that time we can comprehend and actualize personal freedom in a way that cannot be achieved at any other time during the year. It's in the air, ripe for the picking. The same is true of the festival of Succos, which bears the title—*the time of our joy*. If you want to understand what joy is and successfully deal with the inner conflicts that inhibit its expression, then you've got to live in a *succah* for a week. On Succos, the door to the candy store has been left wide open. Whoever wants to can come in and help themselves. Joy is an idea, a state of mind and a challenge. Joy is a tool for living, and on Succos it's there to be better understood and more fully integrated into the fabric of your being.

Rosh Hashanah and Yom Kippur

If you've been to Paris but you missed the Louvre, then you haven't been to Paris. If you participate in a Jewish holiday and you're not different as a result, if you haven't grown, then you have missed the whole point of the holiday.

Rosh Hashanah and Yom Kippur, like all Jewish holidays, are enormous opportunities for personal growth. There is almost no limit to what you can achieve on these days.

It is no wonder that the month of Elul, the month before Rosh Hashanah, is viewed as a month of preparation for the days of Rosh Hashanah and Yom Kippur. The quality of any trip will in large part be a reflection of the preparation put in ahead of time. So it is with the High Holidays, these days of awe—of awesome opportunity for insight and growth.

This is the purpose of the *Rosh Hashanah Yom Kippur Survival Kit*. It has been written to give you an appreciation of what can be accomplished on these days. Admittedly it only begins to scratch the surface. But you must know—even this surface is so fertile, so rich in possibilities for growing, for becoming a more fully developed human being and Jew—that years can be spent harvesting the bounty of this spiritual topsoil. Beneath it lie riches beyond our wildest dreams.

Rosh Hashanah and Yom Kippur are a personal odyssey. The *machzor*—the High Holiday prayer book—serves as the primary guide for this odyssey, and though it is extensively detailed, it outlines only the most important landmarks. Each of these landmarks resides within each and every one of us. They come in the form of questions that ask us what we want to achieve with our lives, as statements of values that give us cause to stop and reflect or as bits of spiritual inspiration. They ask us to rethink our inner lives and the implications of the choices we have made. Each prayer, each internal landmark, calls us away from the stagnation that the routine of life breeds and urges us to reassert our determination that life will always be an exciting quest for understanding and personal development.

There is something enthralling about watching children traverse the path of discovery and growth. However, as the years pass and the less children seem to grow and develop, the less attention we adults pay them. But the thrill of growth doesn't end when we reach voting age. For mature, sensitive, thinking adults, Rosh Hashanah and Yom Kippur contain the tools that will help ensure that our lives continue to blossom and develop long after our shoe sizes reach their outer limits.

A Word about Judaism

Judaism makes demands. It is anything but a religion of comfort. The *Shulchan Aruch* (the code for Jewish living) opens with the statement that, *in the morning a person should rise with the vitality of a lion.*

Let's be honest. When was the last time you felt like a lion in the morning—ready to attack the new day with every ounce of vitality you possessed?

How precious they are, so rarified, those moments when we feel that there is nothing we would rather do than confront life and its challenges head-on. More likely, if you're like most of us, your first impulse upon awakening in the morning is to hit that beloved snooze button and roll over for another twenty minutes of dream-filled bliss.

Together, Rosh Hashanah and Yom Kippur are the dawning moments of a new year. They are 365 mornings all rolled into three days of directed energy. If you feel like rolling over and going back to sleep (after all, you've been through these holidays before), I beg of you, don't. These three days, like Judaism and Jewish life itself, call us to transcend our first inclinations and to strive for a greatness we so long to achieve but are so hesitant to pursue. Rosh Hashanah and Yom Kippur, like life, will take a great deal of effort, perhaps even some pain.

But isn't that what you will teach your children? That the pursuit of comfort is the antithesis of the search for excellence? That if you want to achieve anything of enduring value in life, it will take great determination and effort?

Do your ears hear what your lips speak? The truth about life is so very plain. The challenges—and the rewards—so incredibly enormous. If only we could get out of bed.

Here then is the *Rosh Hashanah Yom Kippur Survival Kit*. Its aim is far more than its title—survival. It is my hope that with the help of this book you will not only survive your experience in synagogue this year but also emerge from the holidays with a new appreciation for the thrilling challenge called life.

ROSH HASHANAH

THE FOREST

SURVIVAL KIT USER'S

GUIDE

—3—

The *Rosh Hashanah Yom Kippur Survival Kit* has been designed to help make these holidays—their prayers, themes and symbols—come alive for you. Here are a few suggestions that will help you get the most out of this book.

1) Sometime before the holidays—

A) Leaf through the material in this book and familiarize yourself with the contents.

B) During the month before Rosh Hashanah read the essays in chapters 7, 9, 12, 13, 14, 17 and 20. These essays explain many primary intellectual and spiritual concepts that will help you develop a personalized perspective and approach to the holidays.

C) You may wish to read these essays—or any part of the Survival Kit—together with family or friends. In past years people have used the book as a focal point for informal study groups and have found that the discussion generated in these groups has led to a deeper appreciation of the holidays and their inherent potential.

D) Look at your *machzor* (High Holiday prayer book) and put a check (✓) on the pages where there are corresponding comments in the Survival Kit. This will allow you to use your *machzor* and this book in an integrated fashion.

2) Take the Survival Kit with you to synagogue—

A) The Survival Kit is not a prayer book and is not meant to take the place of your *machzor*; rather, it is a supplementary guide that can be used in various ways.

i. Where this Survival Kit comments on a prayer, read the comments prior to saying the prayer. The comments are designed to help focus your thoughts on one or two themes within a particular prayer.

ii. If the formality of the service gets to be a bit cumbersome, you can change pace by reading one of the essays in the Survival Kit.

B) Synagogue is a place for reflection as well as prayer. Some of the questions, issues and ideas covered in the Survival Kit can serve as useful guideposts for meaningful introspection.

HOW TO SURVIVE
SYNAGOGUE

—4—

But Rabbi, even if I can read some of the prayers, I still
don't understand what I'm saying…To tell you the truth, I'd
rather take a quiet reflective walk in the park this year than
spend all that time in synagogue saying a bunch of words that
don't really mean much to me anyway.

Prayer is meant to be a powerful, relevant and meaningful experience. At the same time, a lengthy synagogue experience can be a bit intimidating. The following is a list of perspectives to keep in mind this year that should help to make the services as personally uplifting as possible.

1) Five minutes of prayer said with understanding, feeling and a personal connection to the words and their significance means far more than five hours of lip service. Therefore, don't look at your prayer book as an all-or-nothing proposition

consisting of hundreds of prayers that absolutely must be recited. Rather, try looking at each page as its own self-contained opportunity for prayer, reflection and inspiration. If you are successful with one page that's great; if not, then just move right along to the next page, the next of many opportunities.

2) "Self-imposed expectations lead to self-induced frustrations." Therefore, don't expect to be "moved" by every prayer or to follow along with the entire service.

3) Read slowly through the prayers, carefully thinking about what you're saying, and don't be concerned about lagging behind the congregation. Look, the worst that could happen is that you will be on a different page than everyone else, but don't worry, the pages will probably be announced so you can always catch up.

4) If a particular sentence or paragraph touches you, linger there a while. Say the words over and over to yourself—softly, but audible to your own ear. Allow those words to touch you. Feel them. And if you're really brave, then close your eyes and say those words over and over for a couple of moments.

5) You're not that proficient in Hebrew? Don't worry, God understands whatever language you speak. And like a loving parent, He can discern what's in your heart even if you can't quite express it the way you would like.

6) As you sit in your synagogue on Rosh Hashanah and Yom Kippur you are joined by millions of Jews in synagogues all over the world. You are a Jew, and by participating in the holidays you are making a powerful statement about your commitment to Judaism and the Jewish people.

ASK A JEW A QUESTION...

—5—

Jewish thinking relates to holidays as far more than commemorations of past events. Rosh Hashanah is certainly more than a Jewish January first.

The essential opportunity of Rosh Hashanah is to clarify for ourselves what our truest, "bottom line" priorities are in life. No time is more appropriate than today for asking ourselves some basic questions in order to clarify—and remind ourselves—what is truly important to us and who we ultimately want to be.

To reflect on some of the following questions is quite apropos on this, the day of judgment:

1) When do I most feel that my life is meaningful?
2) How often do I express my feelings to those who mean the most to me?
3) Are there any ideals I would be willing to die for?
4) If I could live my life over, would I change anything?

5) What would bring me more happiness than anything else in the world?

6) What are my three most significant achievements since last Rosh Hashanah?

7) What are the three biggest mistakes I've made since last Rosh Hashanah?

8) What project or goal, if left undone, will I most regret next Rosh Hashanah?

9) If I knew I couldn't fail, what would I undertake to accomplish in life?

10) What are my three major goals in life?
   ◆ What am I doing to achieve them?
   ◆ What practical steps can I take in the next two months toward these goals?

11) If I could give my children only three pieces of advice, what would they be?

12) What is the most important decision I need to make this year?

13) What important decision did I avoid making last year?

14) What did I do last year that gave me the strongest feeling of self-respect?

15) When do I feel closest to God?

16) Do I have a vision of where I want to be one, three and five years from now?

17) What are the most important relationships in my life?
   ◆ Over the last year did those relationships become closer and deeper or was there a sense of stagnation and drifting?
   ◆ What can I do to nurture those relationships this year?

18) If I could change only one thing about myself, what would that be?

19) If I could change one thing about my spiritual life, what would it be?

On a scale of one to five (five being the highest), how important are the following to you? You cannot have more than three fives or three fours, and you must have at least two threes, two twos and two ones.

1) Family
2) Being well educated
3) Making a contribution to my community
4) Marriage
5) Spirituality
6) Being well liked
7) Having a good reputation
8) Financial success
9) Being Jewish
10) Peer recognition in my career or profession
11) Personal fulfillment
12) Helping other people
13) Having a good Jewish education
14) Making a contribution to humanity
15) Achieving peace of mind
16) Having children
17) Living in the home of my dreams
18) Acquiring self-knowledge
19) Giving my children a strong Jewish identity

These questions can also be used at your family's holiday meals to create great conversation. Try going around the table and asking everyone to respond to one of the questions.

SEVEN QUESTIONS PEOPLE ASK ABOUT ROSH HASHANAH

—6—

(I)

Question: Why don't we celebrate New Year's in January?

Answer: The calendar that begins in January and ends in December is known as the Gregorian calendar and was introduced by Pope Gregory XIII in 1582. This calendar is based on an even earlier calendar, the Julian calendar, that was introduced by Julius Caesar in 46 B.C.

The Jewish calendar not only is of much earlier origin but also differs from the Gregorian calendar in numerous ways.

1) The Jewish calendar is based on the moon (lunar) and not the sun (solar).

2) The Jewish calendar contains a number of "new year" dates. This is like having a fiscal year that overlaps two calendar years. The month of *Tishrei*, which begins with Rosh Hashanah, is the beginning of the year vis-à-vis the number of years, e.g., 5752,

5753, etc. The month of *Nissan*, the month in which Passover falls, is considered the beginning of the year with regard to the festivals (Passover, Shavuos and Succos) as well as for the establishment of the reign of a Jewish king.

Insight: Our calendar is based on the moon, and similarly the Jewish people are compared to the moon. No matter how dark life seems for the Jewish people, we must know that the "light" is already waiting to reappear. Jewish history is an ongoing portrayal of this principle. Also, unlike the sun, which is always present in its fullest form, the moon progresses in stages until it is full and radiant.

A Jew must look at life as a constant process of growth and development. Tiny beginnings can grow to their fullest potential, and even darkness can be overcome.

(II)

Question: On Chanukah the *menorah* burned for eight days; on Passover the Jews left Egypt. What happened on Rosh Hashanah?

Answer: The Talmud relates that Man was created on the first of Tishrei. This being the case, Rosh Hashanah is a birthday of sorts for the human race.

Insight: In the Torah, the account of the creation of the first human beings states that Man was created, "in the image of God." Jewish tradition understands "the image of God" to mean that human beings possess free will. Our actions are not predetermined by any Divine, psychological or sociological forces; rather, we are free to choose and are thus responsible for the consequences of our actions. As will be explained later, on Rosh Hashanah we celebrate our humanity by exercising our free will.

Life is a gift. You appeared. You had nothing to do with it whatsoever. You had nothing to do with the color of your eyes, the color of your hair, the color of your skin, or how tall you were going to be. You stand with this gift of yourself. What are you going to do with it? God gave you self, gave you life, and gave you the world to live in. What are you going to do with that gift?

Millard Fuller, Founder of Habitat for Humanity[1]

(III)

Question: Is Rosh Hashanah a happy day or a sad day?

Answer: Rosh Hashanah is a happy day, a festival, and at the same time it is a very serious day. It is a serious day because it is the day of judgment, and it is a happy day because we are confident that if we understand the meaning of the day and use it properly, then we will indeed receive a favorable judgment.

(IV)

Question: Why does God judge us?

Answer: Because life is serious business. If we feel that we are being judged, we are more apt to treat life with the proper gravity.

Insight: Big God cares about little me. Judgment implies caring. If you don't care, you don't judge. Therefore, another way of understanding how Rosh Hashanah is both solemn and joyous is seeing God's judgment, the fact that He cares about how we live our lives, as the surest sign of His love.

(V)

Question: Why do we dip an apple in honey?

Answer: Because it tastes good! Also, because it represents our heartfelt wishes for a sweet year, not only for ourselves and our families but also for all the Jewish people.

Insights: 1) On most fruit trees the leaves appear before the fruit, thus providing a protective cover for the young fruit. The apple, however, makes a preemptive move by appearing before the leaves. The Jewish people are compared to an apple because we are willing to live out our Jewish lives even if this seems to leave us unprotected. We have confidence that God and the instructions in the Torah could never mislead us.

2) A bee can inflict pain by its sting, yet it also produces delicious honey. Life has this same duality of potential. We pray that our choices will result in a sweet year.

(VI)

Question: Why do we blow the *shofar*?

Answer: Since Rosh Hashanah is the anniversary of the creation of the world, it follows that it is also the anniversary of God being sovereign over the world. Rosh Hashanah is a coronation of sorts, and thus we trumpet the *shofar* just like at a coronation ceremony.

Insight: In truth, Rosh Hashanah marks the creation of Man, not the world. The actual creation of the world took place five days before the first human beings were created. In Judaism, the creation of the entire universe is marked by celebrating the creation of the purpose of the world: the free-willed human being.

The word *shofar* is related to the Hebrew word, *l'shaper*. The word *l'shaper* means "to beautify." The call of the *shofar* reminds us each of our own calling, the calling to live beautiful lives. Why does our King decree the celebration of holidays and the performance of *mitzvot*, commandments? Only as a way to guide us in the process of beautifying ourselves and the world we live in.

(VII)

Question: If you don't have a *shofar*, will a trumpet or some other instrument suffice?

Answer: No. Our sages teach us that it is specifically a ram's horn that must be used. The ram's horn is an allusion to the binding of Isaac that took place on Rosh Hashanah, when a ram eventually replaced Isaac on the altar.

Insight: Abraham and Isaac, each in his own way, were prepared to give up everything for what they believed was right—the will of their Creator. When we hear the sound of the ram's horn on Rosh Hashanah, we are supposed to consider what sacrifices we would make for what we believe in as Jews.

♦ If things looked dire, would we go fight for Israel?

♦ Would we pass up a good job opportunity if it meant living in a place where our children's Jewish education would be compromised?

◆ Would we give up a week's pay if it were required to help resettle Soviet Jews in Israel?

◆ If hiding our Jewish identity would help us get the job, promotion or date we want, would we hide it?

TAKE A WALK, BREAK-UP A STONE, LISTEN TO THE MUSIC, ACT LIKE A TREE AND GROW

— 7 —

Rosh Hashanah and Yom Kippur are celebrations of human potential. As such, they highlight our ability to grow as human beings and as Jews; they challenge us to develop our nascent capabilities, urge us to reflect on areas of stagnation, demand that we honestly confront our mistakes and insist that change is not only possible but is also in our hands.

One of the great Chassidic masters describes the human being as "forms wrapped within forms", and life as a process of constantly uncovering hidden forms and bringing them out of potential into realization.

It is my hope that some of the thoughts contained in this chapter help bring the potential of these wonderful holidays within your reach and help you to nurture your own potential and bring it out into the light of actualization where it can shine brightly.

(I)

For the human being is a tree in the field.

The Torah

And he shall be like a tree planted by streams of water...

King David

The primary fruits of great people are their acts of goodness.

Early Jewish sages

An angel is called "the one who stands." Man is called "the one who walks."

Jewish mysticism

Judaism finds the unique beauty of human beings in our ability to grow, to bear fruit and to walk and walk and walk. It is part of our nature to strive and to grow. A voice from deep within us calls us to keep moving, keep trying, keep going forward. At the same time, there is nothing easier in life than complacency. In the Jewish view, there is also nothing less human. A cut flower shares its beauty, but only for a while, and it never grows again.

In truth, there are only two human tendencies. The desire to grow and to soar spiritually and the urge to take a long nap.

Rosh Hashanah is a time to look again at ourselves as growers. To remember that as long as there is life there is opportunity. That within us all lie worlds of potential new life—even new lives—that are waiting to be nourished and cultivated. Rosh Hashanah is the antithesis of stagnation, complacency and surrender. When the *shofar* sounds it is meant to rouse us. To focus our attention on the fact that today is a brand new beginning. A chance to start again. A fresh opportunity to set out down the a fertile path of growth. Rosh Hashanah is a day that celebrates the only being in the universe who walks, grows and bears fruit.

As a young boy, Dan Berman was noticeably bright and witty, even at the age of six. You could see the wanderlust in his eyes. At the age of twenty, after completing two years of college in just two semesters and after a ten-month stint as a bar-tender and fill-in piano player at a small jazz club, Dan hugged his disappointed parents farewell.

His search for wisdom took him to Burma, the mysterious Bosnian mountains, Jerusalem and Harvard.

By the time he was fifty, Dan was the semi-retired CEO of a small airline that had been bought by one of the "big boys." His passions were Sun Tzu, Plato, the history of metaphysics, Steven Covey, Starbucks and cross country skiing. For his son, he wanted everything.

Dan sent his son, whom he affectionately referred to as Mr. Magic, off to learn from the world's wisest and most gifted teachers. More than anything else, for his son, he wanted wisdom.

One day, after many years of study and accomplishment, Mr. Magic came home to visit his father. "Please," his father peacefully requested, "take that stone up to your old bedroom." The stone that Dan pointed to looked like it had just been lifted off some sun-baked Arizona mountain; and it easily weighed over three hundred pounds. Although he tried and tried, Dan's son could not work his magic. And he became confused and depressed.

"Son," his father said when he returned, "Have I ever asked of you the impossible?" "Go ahead, break it into pieces and then take it upstairs"[2]

Sometimes our lives seem like immovable objects. The feeling of being overwhelmed comes easily. We want to grow, to move in new directions, to change—but it all seems to be too much. Too heavy of a task.

There is an essential attitude that needs to be in place in order for one to be able to grow and to attempt significant, meaningful changes in life. This is the piece-by-piece attitude.

On the one hand, Rosh Hashanah is inspiring and invigorating as it calls upon us to shake off the dust of unrealized goals and unfulfilled dreams. From the vantage point of Rosh Hashanah we are able to capture a fresh spirit that encourages us to pursue all that is deeply meaningful to us in life; and we have a sense that it is yet within our grasp.

On the other hand, this can all be a bit overwhelming. "Oh come on," A voice within us says, "Quit dreaming, get your feet back on the ground and try being realistic about things." And of course, there is some truth in what that voice is saying. However, it is only a half-truth.

The truth is that we can't achieve everything we want all at once and to attempt to do so will surely overwhelm us. This is why the piece-by-piece attitude is an important starting point for any attempt at growth. At the same time, we must never quit dreaming. And that is why we have Rosh Hashanah—to make sure we begin every year with a dream. And to encourage us not only to dream but also to transform those dreams into growth, piece-by-piece; and to walk, step-by-step; and to bear fruit.

(II)

Let's do lunch.

Anonymous

Choose Life.

God

Life is not something that just is. It is not something you happen to possess as a by product of your birth and your health.

Life is far more than just the collection of certain biological functions in a particular organism. To relate to life as simply a biological state of being, the state of being alive, is to relegate the potential of human existence to something that is not only static, but something over which we have ultimately little or no control.

Life is something you do. As in "Let's do lunch."

Life is dynamic and fluid and malleable.

Life is something you choose—and create.

Human beings are the only living creatures with the ability to choose life.

As we mentioned earlier (p.36) Rosh Hashanah is a birthday of sorts. According to our tradition this is the day on which the first human beings were given life. And as Jewish wisdom understands it, the purpose and challenge of the gift of being alive, is the opportunity to choose life. On Rosh Hashanah, the way we celebrate being alive is by choosing life.

(III)

Do not say, "when I have the time, then I will study,"
because you may never have the time.

Hillel

The task is not yours to complete, yet you are not free
to do nothing.

Rabbi Tarfon

Two of life's most pervasive maladies are chronic procrastination and lingering all-or-nothingness. The legendary sages Hillel and Rabbi Tarfon have some advice for all of us.

When he says, "Do not say, 'when I have the time...' Hillel is implying that the definition of procrastination is the belief that both the present and the future are equally viable times for doing whatever happens to be in front of us. "Look," we often tell ourselves, "if I don't do it today, I'll get to it tomorrow." And then somehow, tomorrow never comes.

The future is a paradox. You can't make choices in the future and you can't grow or change or achieve things in the future. You can talk about the future, you can plan for the future, you can dream about the future but you can only choose and do and grow and live in the present. Hillel's prescription for procrastination is to realize that life takes place in the present tense and that we need to live as if the future is not an option.

From a certain perspective, Rosh Hashanah is an exercise in living in the present (see p. 65). And by living in the present we acknowledge that the surest way to mold and shape our future is to pretend that it doesn't exist. This is not an "Eat, drink and be merry for tomorrow we may die" attitude; rather, it is a "Choose at least one bit of growth today, or I may never grow at all" attitude.

And now for Rabbi Tarfon: Rabbi Tarfon, like Hillel, wants us to think and live in the present tense, but with an added twist. Rabbi Tarfon is urging us to focus more on engaging the opportunities of life that are in front of us now and less on the potential of some future final result.

This means that we need to adjust our goals from being achievement oriented to being effort oriented. That we must abandon the type of thinking that says; if I can't achieve everything then why bother at all? Rabbi Tarfon is telling us that while we need goals and dreams, at the same time we must be prepared to make any efforts we can even if they seem to represent only partial successes or half-fulfilled dreams. Life is not an all-or-nothing affair.

The only thing that is always in our hands is our ability to make an effort; to try, to take at least one step forward and to act upon whatever opportunity presents itself to us. To make an attempt at change, to try to grow and to try to achieve our goals; this we can always do. The ultimate achievement, however, is often impacted by people and factors beyond our control, not the least of which is God.

This, I believe, is the prescription that Hillel and Rabbi Tarfon are offering. The way to be a success in the future is to forget about the future, engage the present and try to do something meaningful today. Then, by choosing a little bit of meaning each day, you will find that when the future does arrive you will have done all that you possibly could to insure that your future is one that you can feel good about.

(IV)

When it comes to the most important things in life, we all have a form of attention deficit disorder.

Sam

Stand still and see!

Moses, just before the sea split

When I was growing up, it often happened that I would misplace things, sometimes expensive things, and that didn't exactly go over big with my parents. After combing my bedroom or the backyard for whatever it was I had misplaced, I would slink into the kitchen and sheepishly declare to my mother, "It's not there, I looked everywhere." And my mother's reply was always the same: "Sam, go look again; and this time look with your eyes open." And guess what? I almost always found what I was looking for.

Picture this scene: You and two million other Jews have just been liberated from bondage in Egypt. You've been in the desert for a week, Pharaoh has decided he wants you back, you and the entire Israelite nation are camping out at the edge of the sea and the Egyptian army is barreling down on you. Yikes! You are really hoping that Moses has one more good plague up his sleeve. And, thank God, he does. Moses climbs up on a big rock by the edge of the sea, the wind blowing at his back, he lifts his staff and addresses the entire Jewish nation. (Somebody should make a movie out of this.) "Stand still and see," he tells the people. "God Himself is about to rescue you..."

Stand still and see. What's that supposed to mean? And what if they wouldn't stand still; would they then not be able to see something? I mean this is the splitting of the sea; who could miss that even if they weren't standing still?

What Moses was teaching the Jewish people at that moment was that it is possible to witness an event but not see what took place. Moses didn't just want them to notice that the sea had split, he wanted them to see. To perceive, to ponder and to absorb the experience and its meaning. He wanted that event to make a profound and lasting impression on them, and for that, they would have to stand still. Only then would they be able to truly see what was taking place.

Judaism asserts that the ability to stand still is a delicate and invaluable discipline that opens us up to noticing, appreciating and absorbing much of the beauty, wonder and wisdom of life. Wonder that is all around us but which we rarely see because we don't know how to stand still and pay attention.

Rosh Hashanah affords us an opportunity to stand still—and to see. Often, because we are so busy living, we lose sight of what we're doing and why we're doing it; of where we're going, why are we going there and if is this the course we want our lives to be taking. On Rosh Hashanah we can stand still, look at our lives, see what is taking place and then reflect carefully and consciously on what it is we are seeing. If you do nothing else this Rosh Hashanah, take some time to stand still and see.

(V)

*[A Streetcar Named Desire] Blanche DuBois, sliding
into insanity, is one of the greatest and most challenging roles
available to an actress. In recent years, Ann Margaret lost ten
pounds and grew depressed and anxious playing Blanche.
Jessica Lange got panic attacks.*
National Public Radio, <u>All Things Considered</u>

Constantin Stanislavski developed a system of acting that became so prominent that today it is referred to as simply The Method. Marlon Brando, Ann Bancroft and Paul Newman are just a few of the more well-known method actors.

Stanislavski detected a profound relationship between the human spirit and the body. He taught that the careful altering of body motions and the conscious directing of the mind's thoughts could actually change a person's chemistry and have a dramatic effect on feelings and emotions. Recently, researchers studying an actor playing a depressing role and then later a part from an <u>I Love Lucy</u> episode reported that "data suggested that there was a correlation between the type of personality being performed and immune responsiveness."[3]

*External movements have the ability to awaken internal
feelings and emotions. Though feelings often seem to be out of
our control, by consciously acting in a certain way, we can
gain mastery over our feelings.*
Moshe Chaim Luzzatto, 18th century scholar and mystic

Sometimes, when it comes to growth and change, to the attempt at transforming aspects of our lives, it's okay to be a hypocrite. What I mean is this: If you want to be a more patient person but feel you can't because inside you feel quite impatient, then what you can do is act like a patient person even though you don't feel like one. Likewise, you can act the way a loving person would act, act the way a responsible person would act, and so on.

Long ago our tradition taught us what method actors have recently discovered: That playing a superficial role has the power to nurture a deep transformation. This will sound a bit odd, but on Rosh Hashanah and Yom Kippur it is appropriate to choose a role that you want to act out over the coming year and to use your newfound acting career as a vehicle for growth.

(VI)

Listen to the Music.

The Doobie Brothers

*M*r. Segal loves Passover. Yes, he loves conducting the seder, but even more, he loves that his out-of-town children and grandchildren come to spend the entire week of Passover with him and Mrs. Segal. And what a sight the Segal home is for that week. With the in-town grand-children, the out-of-town grandchildren and a few stray kids from the neighborhood all gathering to play in the Segal house, the place resembles—and sounds like—an overcrowded ride at an amusement park more than the modest suburban home that it is.

It was the first Shabbat after Passover and all the out-of-town kids had already packed up their afikomen presents and gone back home. Mr. Segal was sitting in his usual place in synagogue, lost in prayer and thought, when he felt a tap on his shoulder. It was Morty Kaplan.

"It must be nice at home now without all that noise?"

Mr. Segal lifted his head slowly, his peaceful eyes met those of Mr. Kaplan. "Morty, that wasn't noise, that was music."

The next time your child, spouse, sibling, parent or friend does something that you find annoying, think about how fortunate you are to have them in your life, think about how precious they are—and see if you can't hear the music.

Sometimes in life we can change everything just by changing the way we look at things.

(VII)

It is very close to you; it is on your lips, in your heart; so that you will live with it.

The Torah

The Torah presents us with a powerful meditative technique for accessing our potential for spiritual growth. I learned this technique from my teacher in Jerusalem almost twenty years ago; I hope you find it as helpful as I have.

It is very close to you. That which you long for in life is within your reach.

It is on your lips. Put your yearnings, your goals and your dreams into words. Then in a quiet, peaceful tone, say those words over and over to yourself. Let the words fill your mind and permeate your being until they are...

In your heart. Allow those words to be transformed into stirring emotions.

So that you will live with it. Give those emotions a place to express themselves in the realm of action; in the way you live.

Throughout the rest of the Survival Kit, you will find suggestions for verbal meditations. You can experiment with as many as you wish, and it is certainly appropriate for you to construct your own phrases to contemplate.

The meditations will always be recognizable because of the way they are set off from the text of the book. The first two appear here. Go ahead, give them a try. Let the words be on your lips; and in your heart.

1) I long to express the deepest parts of who I am; and I will find a way.

2) Perfection is an illusion; I seek only to grow.

HIGHLIGHTS OF THE ROSH HASHANAH MORNING SERVICE

—8—

Birchas HaShachar—Morning Blessings

Asher Yatzar / Who Has Designed Man with Wisdom

Blessed are you God, who has designed man with wisdom and created many openings and tubes...if but one of them were to be ruptured it would be impossible to survive...

> *You've got 75 trillion cells, and a lot of those cells are reproducing while we're talking; they're replicating their DNA—huge long strands of millions of bunches of little submolecules called nucleotides. It can't happen perfectly; there are mistakes. So cruising up and down the*

> *DNA molecule are a bunch of patrol boats: DNA-repair enzymes. They see an error and they grab it, snip it out, and fix it. While we've been talking, that has probably happened a few thousand times in each of us. I hate to use clichés, but that really does boggle the mind. And this sophisticated coordination happens at the molecular level, the organ level—the whole body is a unity, and the purpose of the unity is to keep us alive.[4]*

Intel—move over.

In this prayer we focus on the wonder of our bodily functions. The complexity and fragility are equally humbling.

Birchas HaTorah / Blessings for the Torah

The Torah is a set of instructions for living. It contains wisdom, moral teachings and commandments. Insight, guidelines and guidance.

The Jewish people have been scattered. We speak various languages and come in a variety of sizes and colors. We have different opinions, different practices and an endless collage of customs.

All that we have in common is the Torah. It is what binds us with each other today and with the Jews of decades and centuries gone by. The more we probe the Torah for life's insights, the more we study—and study together—the closer we will become. In these blessings we thank God for commanding us to be involved in the study of the Torah.

Aylu Devarim / These Matters Have No Set Measure

On the night of the Passover seder there is a *mitzva* (a commandment) to eat matzah. But a nibble won't do; there is a minimum prescribed amount that must be eaten. Similarly, many other observances are limited to specific "measures," specific amounts.

This is not so, however, when it comes to acts of human compassion and kindness or to developing a relationship with God or pursuing the wisdom stored in our Torah.

For these life defining essentials we must use our own best judgment. For those elements that determine the tone of our life's involvements, we are the final arbiters of priority. How highly this speaks of our ability and integrity. How weighty this renders our responsibility.

Elokai Neshama / **The Soul**

Save the whales, save the spotted owl or save a human being. Which one takes precedence? Are any of these lives more valuable than the others?

Consider this: if the essential difference between a man and an animal lies in the realm of intelligence, then is human life more valuable than animal life just because we happen to be smarter?

At this point in the morning service we focus on the fact that there is something else, another part of us that separates us from our pets. It is that part of us that stands in awe, transfixed by a brilliant sunset or by the waves coming to shore in the dead of night. It is that part of us—our soul—that longs to transcend the mundane and to touch the spirit of life, the essence, the Divine.

Brachos / **Morning Blessings**

> *Blessed are You...who gives sight to the blind...clothes to the naked...enables me to walk...*

Never have so many wanted so much and found so little.

Happiness is the true treasure of living. And, "Who is wealthy?" our sages asked. "He who takes pleasure in what he has."

The prayer book reminds us to be thankful for *all* we have.

Our eyes and our ears. Our friends and our family. Our homes, our cars, our health and yes, even our ability to get out of bed in the morning and stand on our own two feet.

Shacharis—The Morning Service

HaMelech / The King

On Rosh Hashanah we proclaim God as king—our sovereign ruler as well as our judge.

A child does not have to be beaten to be abused. To ignore a child so that she feels you aren't interested and don't care is terrible abuse. Such a child would rather be yelled at—even punished—than ignored.

The existence of a day of judgment means that God is interested in us. He cares. What we do *does* ultimately matter.

Hamayir L'aretz / He Illuminates the Earth

Each day He brings the universe into existence. How vast are all Your creations…fashioned in wisdom…

Imagine if you could have witnessed creation itself. Everyday is an opportunity to take a fresh look at the awesome wonders that surround us. To listen to the wind, the rain and the birds' song. To see the beauty of a gentle cloud, a creek, the trees and—

Ahava Raba / You Have Loved Us Abundantly

For some reason it always seems easier to complain than to be thankful, to focus on what we don't have rather than on what we do have.

Face your deficiencies and acknowledge them; but do not let them master you. Let them teach you patience, sweetness, insight…Use your eyes as if tomorrow you would be stricken blind. Smell the perfume of flowers, taste with relish each morsel, as if tomorrow you could never smell and taste again.

Helen Keller

For just a moment focus on those aspects of your life that are so very good, that enrich your existence; and feel the love.

The Shema / **Hear O' Israel**

> *This is the sadness at the heart of our secular lives. No one wants to live in a pointless, chaotic cosmos, but that is the one that science has given us, and that our culture has largely championed. We may yearn for the divine, but our feet are stuck in the moral relativism (or even nihilism) that such a culture breeds. The post-modern Dadaism that's hip today is the best we can do; everything's a joke.*

Marty Kaplan, <u>New York Times</u> Op-Ed page[5]

Sartre's first major work was entitled *Nausea*, because that is what one must feel if one stares an accidental and meaningless existence in the face.

Shema Yisroel! A Jew lives to teach the world that there is a God. That our existence is not an odd fluke, but rather a deeply meaningful experience. That life is a precious gift and that there is an eternal and transcendent dimension to reality.

> *When I went to the moon I was as pragmatic a test pilot, engineer and scientist as any of my colleagues. But when I saw the planet Earth floating in the vastness of space…the presence of divinity became almost palpable and I knew that life in the universe was not just an accident.*

Edgar Mitchell, 1971 Apollo 14 astronaut

Amidah—The Standing Prayer

The *Amidah* is commonly referred to as the silent prayer. This, however, is a misnomer, for the *Amidah* is to be said softly, not silently, to yourself. The words should be audible to your ears and your ears alone. To your heart and your heart alone.

Far too often the Jewish people have been faced with despair. But rather than wither we have responded with hope, with courage and even with joy and optimism.

Much of the *Amidah* is an expression of our longing for a better, more humane world.

Hashem Sefasai Tiftach / God Open My Lips

A toddler thinks that she cannot walk, but she can. A child fears he will never swim, but he will. Each of us is aware of our abilities and potential, and we all experience fear, doubt and hesitation. Many of our limitations in life are more perceived than real. Often, it is only phantoms that are holding us back.

In Hebrew the word for lips is the same as the word for *banks*, as in river banks. The banks of a river define its limits. When we say "God, open my lips," we are also saying, "God, help me to see beyond my perceived limitations. Help me to see all the way to the horizon of my potential."

> 3) I will create time in my life to nurture my soul.
> 4) Life is a gift I received; I will find a way to "give something back."

Man: Microcosm of the Universe

God created two worlds: One of immense proportions and another equally vast, though not manifestly so.

In Hebrew the word for world, or universe, is *olam*. The universe is referred to as *olam hagadol*, the macro-universe. Man is known to our sages as *olam hakatan*, the micro-universe. The word *olam* also has another connotation: it means concealment. The fullness of what is contained in an *olam*, a universe, is not always apparent.

Man, microcosm of the universe that he is, is the keeper of a potential that borders on the infinite. On one level this thought defies our comprehension, while in the same instance it is clearly understood. We all wonder if there is anything that lies beyond the reach of human beings.

Each and every one of us is a unique *olam*, a universe of potential. One minute you see it and the next it seems to vanish. Our potential stretches as far as the eye can see.

Zachreynu L'Chaim / Remember Us for Life

The voice was that of one who survived the unfathomable hell of Auschwitz. A silent terror still lines his face—even when he smiles.

"If I had a choice," he said, "of having to relive every torturous moment again or to be a German guard in the camps, I'd go through it all again rather than serve for even one hour as a guard."

The German guards lived and breathed. They went home to wives and children, they enjoyed the finest classical music and they laughed: All in a day's work. But they were dead.

The life that we ask for and strive for on Rosh Hashanah is more than just survival. It's a life of value and meaning. You can be alive and dead or you can be alive and live. Choose life!

Magen Avraham / Shield of Abraham

There is, they say, a spark of Abraham in all of us. Abraham, the founder of the Jewish nation, was one man in a very foreign world. No one—literally no one—thought the way he did. No one shared his values, his vision, his dedication to meaningful actions.

Each of us is the fusion of body and soul, physical and spiritual. At times it seems the soul is so alone, forever lost in the fatty recesses of the body, in the murky world of materialism.

In Yiddish there is a particular term for the special spark in every Jewish soul, it's known as the *pintele yid* (the Jewish essence). This *pintele yid*, this essence, is a deep part of every Jew, a longing that can never be extinguished. A bit of light, no matter how dim, forever shines.

The miracle of the exodus of Russian Jews to Israel is not so much that they are finally free, not so much that there even exists an Israel to receive them, but that by the thousands and hundreds of thousands they still care very much about being Jewish. Seventy years of relentless physical and psychological oppression was unable to extinguish the Abraham—that spark in the Jewish soul.

*A*n Israeli newspaper reported that tens of thousands of recent Russian immigrants, children and adults, have received a bris mila (circumcision) upon their arrival in Israel. Many of these take place in almost assembly line fashion with the mohel performing one after another. A newspaper reporter was questioning the immigrants waiting in line about the motivation for their actions. When asked if he believed in God, one middle-aged Russian who was raised on a steady diet of Communist propaganda declared, "No, I don't believe in God, I'm an atheist." The curious reporter, a bit taken aback, went on, "Then why are you having a bris?" There in the land of Israel, the land of King David and the Maccabees, of the Western Wall and Ethiopian Jews, the Russian answered proudly, "Without a bris, it is impossible to be a Jew!"

Only a Jewish atheist could utter such words, and only the spark of Abraham could yield such an atheist.

U'Vchayn Tayn Pach'dcha / Instill Awe and Fear

There aren't many injuries in BASE jumping. You either live or you die.

Frank Gambalie, expert BASE jumper

I expect to lose three to four friends a year.

Nancy Prichard, prominent ice climber[6]

Did you ever notice how people will pay good money to be frightened? Millions of people visit amusement parks each year. And where do you find the longest lines? At the roller coaster: a ride that tries to convince you that your next moment will be your last.

A brush with death is exhilarating. In an article about extreme sports, U.S. News & World Report observed that, "many athletes go to the extreme because they feel most vibrantly alive when straddling the line between safety and danger." If you've ever had a "close call" in a car then you know that you were far more alert and alive after the narrow escape than you were the entire day before.

In Hebrew the word for fear is *yira*, which also means to see or to perceive. If you choose to see life for what it is, an enormous opportunity and a serious responsibility, rather than look the other way, well, that can be frightening—or exhilarating.

U'Vchayn Tzadikim / The Righteous Will See and Be Glad

Far too often the Jewish people have come face to face with utter despair. Surely history would pardon us if we succumbed to despondency and lethargy in the face of this relentless confrontation.

Yet we have chosen to do otherwise. We have responded with optimism and hope, even where there seemed to be none, with quiet courage and with joy. You read the newspapers, day in and day out, and you long for a more humane world. We believe that it is possible—despite the headlines.

Avinu Malkeinu / **Our Father Our King**

A father has a very special love for each and every one of his children but not necessarily the means to give them everything he wants to give.

An omnipotent king looks out from his palace and sees a nation—faceless individuals he will never know.

There are moments in Jewish history when we sense both *Avinu*, our Father and *Malkeinu*, our King.

A high-tech war in the Persian Gulf brought down a shower of missiles on a largely undefended Israel. In such a scenario, Israeli military experts predicted, hundreds if not thousands would be lost.

Avinu Malkeinu, hundreds of residential buildings were reduced to rubble and yet there was scarcely a casualty.

5) The love I feel for my (sister, husband, daughter, father etc.) is transcendent; I will cherish it forever and seek ways to express it.

6) It is a privilege to be a part of the Jewish people; I will search for ways to deepen that connection.

MORNING TORAH

READINGS

—9—

An Overview

The Phenomenon of Jewish Survival (First Day Reading)

How is it that the Jewish people have survived—and why? The greatest of minds, historians and philosophers alike are humbled as they grope for an answer to this enigma of human history.

On the first day of Rosh Hashanah we read about the birth of a son named Isaac to an elderly couple named Abraham and Sarah. A model was established for a pattern in Jewish history. Given the advanced ages of Abraham and Sarah, a child should never have been born, but he was. Given the forces at work against Jewish survival, we simply should not be here, but we are.

The Meaning of Jewish Survival (Second Day Reading)

The purpose of Jewish survival does not lie in some deep-seated desire to be listed in the *Guinness Book of World Records* under the heading "Longest History for a Persecuted People." Rather, the purpose and meaning of our history is to make a difference. To have an impact on how humankind looks at itself and the world it inhabits.

In the midst of civilizations that glorified the warrior and the wars he fought, the prophet Isaiah gave voice to a revolutionary Jewish idea: "Nation shall not lift up sword against nation, neither shall they learn war anymore."

Today, two millennia later, these same words are etched on the facade of the United Nations headquarters. Ask yourself which is more inexplicable: the dogged persistence of this notion in the face of a hostile world or the survival of the people that carried this message in that same oppressive milieu.

How absolutely breathtaking—a depth of commitment that was able to transcend any obstacle, to defy all odds. The events recorded in the second day Torah reading set the stage for this, our ultimate commitment.

The Big Bang Theory of Rosh Hashanah

When was the last time you experienced judgment day? Was it when your boss said to you, "Can you come into my office before you leave today? I'd like to speak with you." Or perhaps you had a court date, a real-life experience of sitting before a judge, being examined and cross-examined, and having to answer for your actions, thoughts and intentions.

How about in your own mind? Perhaps you were lying awake one night or driving alone in a car without the radio on. When you were the court, with everything wrapped up in one mind, one conscience: judge, jury, prosecutor and defendant.

We have all lived through days of judgment—Days when the past has come back to haunt us.

In the Torah portion for the first day of Rosh Hashanah we find the following statement. *And God heard the voice of the young boy, and then an angel of God called to Hagar from heaven and said to her, what is the matter with you Hagar? Do not be afraid, for God has heard the voice of the young boy right where he is.*

When the sages of the Talmud refract this verse through the unique lens of wisdom that is theirs, a mystifying perspective on Rosh Hashanah comes to the fore.

This "young boy" was Yishmael, Abraham's son. Even as a young boy, Yishmael was a cold-blooded murderer. As an adult, he, and his descendants, would be bitter oppressors of the Jewish people.

Yishmael lay there abandoned, left to die. But God caused Hagar to notice a well and she was able to draw water and save the life of Yishmael. Why, Why! That Yishmael had an evil past was well known, that his future would sow seeds of even greater evil and destruction—this was known to God.

At that moment, "right where he is," Yishmael was being judged. Our sages tell us that the dynamics of judgment as they applied to Yishmael apply to us too. On Rosh Hashanah God looks at us *right where we are*. At first blush our sages have given us good reason to breathe a sigh of relief. Think about it. Right where you are! God, though He knows the future, will not take it into account. Fair enough. But listen to this—God won't even take our past into account. All we have to do is get our act together for one day. Say what we are supposed to say, do what we are supposed to do, act the way we are supposed to act and don't worry. The future doesn't count, the past is irrelevant, we will only be judged according to who we are on the day of Rosh Hashanah itself.

Sages or no sages, that doesn't seem to make sense, or for that matter, to be just or right.

We are being asked to pause. To think for a moment and to take a second look at the meaning of Rosh Hashanah as the day of judgment.

So let us do just that. Let us take a second and deeper look at Rosh Hashanah, at judgment and at ourselves.

Current theory regarding the nature of the origin of the universe is commonly referred to as the Big Bang Theory. This theory posits that before the big bang occurred, there was no time, space, matter, or energy. What was there? you may ask. Obviously there was nothing. Well, if there was nothing, how does nothing "explode" in a big bang and become a universe?

What preceded the big bang was an infinitesimally small mathematical point that was not made up of matter, contained no energy, occupied no space, and preceded time itself. Paradoxically, this inconceivably tiny point contained within it the entire universe. This tiny primordial point represents ultimate potential. Whatever it was, when it "exploded" it unleashed an entire universe. From gravity to time and from protons to cockroaches, they were all present in some form before the big bang took place.

Rosh Hashanah is the big bang. On Rosh Hashanah we neither ponder our future nor grapple with our past. On Rosh Hashanah we confront our ultimate potential.

Each one of us is destined to explode. Each one of us, with our lives, will create an entire universe. Each one of us possesses a profoundly immense and unique potential. The question is this: Will the universe we create be a true reflection of the potential we possess?

Rosh Hashanah is the day of judgment. Yet never once during the prayers on Rosh Hashanah do we mention our past or ask for any kind of forgiveness. For this we wait until Yom Kippur. But that's odd. How can we be judged if we don't deal with our past deeds?

The answer is that we all make mistakes in life, mistakes that move us further and further from a realization of our potential as human beings and as Jews. If we are not whole-heartedly committed to pursuing a path to our ultimate potential, then we are inevitably doomed to repeat the mistakes of our past and find new ways to move ever further from our potential. From being the person we truly want to be and *can* be.

And so it is with the dialectic of Rosh Hashanah and Yom Kippur. On Rosh Hashanah we refine the vision of our potential and commit to it. Then and only then can we ensure that the changes we make on Yom Kippur will be of a lasting nature.

There is a famous story about an elderly sage named Reb Zusia. Reb Zusia lay on his deathbed surrounded by his students and disciples. Reb Zusia was crying and there was no one who could comfort him.

One student offered, "You were almost as wise as Moses himself;" another followed saying, "You were almost as kind as our father Abraham;" and so on. Yet Reb Zusia would not be comforted. He wept as the end drew near.

"When I pass from this world and appear before the heavenly tribunal," Reb Zusia said, "they won't ask me, 'Zusia, why weren't you as wise as Moses or as kind as Abraham?' rather they will ask me 'why weren't you Zusia?' Why didn't I fulfill my potential, why didn't I follow the path that could have been mine?"

On Rosh Hashanah we confront our potential as human beings but even more, as Jews. The question is one of commitment. The issue is one of judgment.

> 7) I possess a deep desire to be kind and helpful.
> 8) God cares about me; my life is significant and valuable.

THE SHOFAR SERVICE

—IO—

Prelude to the Shofar

Psalm 47: To He Who Grants Victory

There are only two ways to build the tallest building. One, start building, or two, tear down all the others.

The challenge of life is not unlike that of fashioning a majestic structure. In Jewish thought, this challenge is a forty-nine step process.*

There are only two ways to reach our goals and realize our potential. One is by good old-fashioned dedication and persistence. The other is to redefine our potential as being what we have already achieved. Simple, game over.

We read Psalm 47 seven times. In doing so we mention God's name forty-nine times. We are reminded to set our goals in life high and to keep them there.

---

* The forty-nine days that elapsed between the exodus from Egypt and the receiving of the Torah at Mt. Sinai serve as a paradigm for this forty-nine step growth process. These are the forty-nine days that link the holidays of Passover and Shavuos and are known as the Sefira. Each day during this period is identified by a unique element of potential for personal growth and character development.

A Call for Clarity

The *shofar* is the most recognizable of all the Rosh Hashanah symbols. The sounding of the *shofar* plays a central role in the day's service. Young and old alike gather in a hush to listen carefully to the cry of the *shofar*.

1) The commandment on Rosh Hashanah is "to hear" the sound of the *shofar*. From the *Shema* we learn that "hearing" in Judaism means to understand. The call of the *shofar* is the sound that wakes us up so that we will make a choice for clarity, for awareness, for a fully constructive and purposeful life.

2) The blowing of the *shofar* consists of three sets of three different notes. Thus the minimum number of *shofar* blasts one is required to hear is nine; however, the accepted manner of blowing actually results in many more sounds. Each of the three notes (*Tekiah, Teruah, Shevarim*) is designed to evoke a particular idea and feeling.

Tekiah (long note): This note calls us from the routines of day-to-day living, from a dissipation of our creative energies, to refocus on who it is we truly want to be. The *Tekiah* challenges us to feel the power and the potential of our innermost selves—a part of ourselves we may have lost touch with over the year—and then dares us to commit ourselves to the pursuit of our awesome potential.

Teruah (short note): This note is more comforting. It softens us, allowing us to integrate the thoughts and feelings of the day. The *Teruah* says; before you rush headlong into the new year energized by your rekindled convictions, pause for a moment. Let the sense of inspiration settle in. Let it fill your soul.

Shevarim (medium note): This is an anxious, longing note. Feel the tugging, the yearning to somehow start again, this time accomplishing what we want in life.

3) On the simplest, most basic level the sound of the *shofar* is the muffled cry of an injured soul. A soul crying for freedom. Free to be its own uninhibited self. The homing signal in every Jewish heart.

You That Slumber—Awake! A Shofar Essay

1) Abraham, our forefather, stood on one side of the river and the entire world stood on the other. Abraham, the Midrash tells us, was able to take an unpopular stand against all of humanity. A stand for truth, for meaning, for immutable values, for everything that is right and good. One man against the world. Our sages taught, *"The deeds of the forefathers are a portent for the children."* We, the Jewish people, are the spiritual heirs to the character, and the depth of being that Abraham possessed.

2) The full force of the German people—the German war machine—was brought to bear on the objective of destroying the Jews. Yet somehow, in some inexplicable way, stories of survival and commitment abound. Jews by the thousands and tens of thousands refused to compromise their morality, their commitment to truth and meaning and ultimately their commitment to God, Torah and Judaism. They stood face to face: a tortured and suffering people and all that they stood for, against a mighty and merciless enemy and all that it stood for.

> *The Jews were forced back against the barbed wire. The barbs pierced their flesh, pricking their bones, and the blood began to trickle and run. The Jews huddled and crowded together, stumbling and falling as more kept coming, colliding against the fallen ones and falling with them.*
>
> *In the midst of this confusion the shrieking voice of the murderous chief was heard again:*
>
> *"Sing, arrogant Jews, sing! Sing or you will die! Gunners, aim your machine guns! Now listen, you dirty Jews. Sing or you will die!"*

And at that horrifying moment, one man pried himself loose from the frightened mob and broke the conspiracy of total silence. He stood there all alone and began to sing. His song was a chassidic folk song in which the chassid poured out his soul before the Almighty:

"Lomir zich iberbeiten, iberbeiten,
Avinu shebashamayim,
Lomir zich iberbeiten, iberbeiten, iberbeiten—"
*"Let us be reconciled, our Heavenly Father,
Let us be reconciled, let us make up—"*

A spark of song was kindled, but that spark fell short of its mark. The Jews had been beaten, and recoiled. The voice of the singer did not reach them. His song was silenced. There was no singing.

But something did happen at that moment. A change took place.

As soon as the solitary voice was hushed, humbly, another voice picked up the same tune, the same captivating chassidic tune. Only the words were not the same. New words were being sung. One solitary person in the entire humiliated and downtrodden crowd had become the spokesman of all the Jews. This man had composed the new song on the spot, a song derived from the eternal wellspring of the nation. The melody was the same ancient chassidic melody, but the words were conceived and distilled through the crucible of affliction:

"Mir velen zey iberleben, iberleben,
Avinu shebashamayim,
Mir velen zey iberleben, iberleben, iberleben—"
*"We shall outlive them, our Heavenly Father,
We shall outlive them, outlive them, outlive them—"*

> *This time the song swept the entire crowd. The new refrain struck like lightning and jolted the multitude. Feet rose rhythmically, as if by themselves. The song heaved and swelled like a tidal wave, arms were joined, and soon all the frightened and despondent Jews were dancing.*
>
> *As for the commander, at first he clapped his hands in great satisfaction, laughing derisively. "Ha, ha, ha, the Jews are singing and dancing! Ha, ha, the Jews have been subdued!" But soon he grew puzzled and confused. What is going on? Is this how subdued people behave? Are they really oppressed and humiliated? They all seem to be fired up by this chassidic dance, as if they have forgotten all pain, suffering, humiliation, and despair. They have even forgotten about the presence of the Nazi commander . . .*
>
> *"Stop, Jews! Stop at once! Stop the singing and dancing! Stop! Stop immediately!" the oppressor yelled out in a terrible voice, and for the first time his well-disciplined subordinates saw him at a loss, not knowing what to do next. "Stop! Stop! Stop at once!" the commander pleaded with his soldiers in a croaking voice. The Jews, singing and dancing ecstatically, were swept by the flood of their emotions and danced on and on. They paid a high price for it. They were brutally beaten for their strange behavior. But their singing and dancing did not stop.[7]*

3) The world watched in awe. A tiny man was led across an obscure little bridge. A short walk from bondage to freedom. "From the moment I decided never to make a moral compromise—I was a free man." These were the words of Anatoly Sharansky, one small Jew who made a choice. The choice to stand for truth and for justice—even against the crushing power of his Soviet oppressors.

4) The Jewish people have always taken a stand. For truth. For what is good and right. For pursuing that which we know to be meaningful, no matter where it may lead. Each one of us longs

to take a stand. Deep within us all lies the strength and ability to take that stand. The *shofar* calls out to us. It is a call for clarity. To clarify for ourselves what we ultimately want, who we want to be, what we really want to be committed to. The *shofar* sounds and stirs something deep within our hearts and souls. We can sense the power. On Rosh Hashanah we can achieve the clarity and commitment to stand alone as individuals and together as a people. To take a stand for everything the Jewish people represent. All we have to do is listen.

Wolf Fischelberg and his twelve-year-old son Leo were walking among the barracks of the sector for privileged people (Bevorzugenlager) in Bergen-Belsen, trying to barter some cigarettes for bread. As they were turning into another row of barracks, a stone was thrown across the barbed wire separating one sector from another. The stone flew over their heads and landed at their feet. It was clear that this was aimed at father and son.

"What does it mean?" Wolf turned to his son.

"Nothing! Just an angry Jew hurling stones," replied the son with a defiant note in his tone.

"Angry Jews do not cast stones; it is not part of our tradition," replied the father.

"Maybe it is time that it should become part of our tradition," the son snapped with restrained anger.

Wolf Fischelberg looked around to see if all was clear. Only then did he bend down to pick up the stone. A small gray note was wrapped around it. Wolf slipped the note into his pocket. They walked into a safe barracks where other Polish Jews lived. In a corner at a distance from the others, Wolf read the note. It was written in Hebrew by a Dutch Jew named Hayyim Borack, who had Argentinean papers. After establishing his credentials, Hayyim wrote that he was fortunate to have obtained a shofar and it was in his possession. If the chassidic Jews from the Polish transports wished to use the shofar for Rosh Hashanah services, Borack could smuggle the shofar in one of the coffee cauldrons used in the morning distribution. In doing so they would lose a cauldron of coffee, for the shofar would be covered with a minimal amount of coffee, just enough to conceal it.

A vote was taken among the Polish Jews. Those in favor of the plan to smuggle in the shofar held a clear majority. They agreed to give up their morning coffee ration on the first day of Rosh Hashanah.

At the time and place specified in the note, a stone once more made its way over the electrified barbed-wire, this time from the Polish Jews to the Dutch. "You see, my son, Jews never throw stones in vain," said Wolf, as his eyes followed the stone making its way from one sector to another.

The smuggling of the shofar was a success. Nobody was caught and the shofar was not damaged. But now a new problem arose. In order to fulfill the mitzvah, the obligation of shofar blowing, all present must clearly hear the voice of the shofar. The risk was great. If the sounds of the shofar reached German ears, all present would pay with their lives.

A heated debate developed among the scholars in the barracks as to whether one could properly fulfill the commandment of sounding the shofar if it could not be heard distinctly. In the absence of books, all discussants relied on their memory and quoted precedents from various Jewish sources. Based on Halachah (Jewish law), a decision was reached to blow the shofar quietly. God would surely accept the muffled sounds of the shofar and prayers of His sons and daughters just as He had accepted the prayers of Isaac atop the altar of Mount Moriah, thought Wolf Fischelberg as he was about to blow the shofar.

As little Miriam, Wolf's daughter, listened to the shofar, she hoped that it would bring down the barbed-wire fences of Bergen-Belsen, just as the blasts of the shofar had in earlier times made the walls of Jericho come tumbling down. The service was over. Nothing had changed. The barbed wires remained fixed in their places. Only in the heart did something stir—knowledge and hope: knowledge that the muffled voice of a shofar had made a dent in the Nazi wall of humiliation and slavery, and hope that someday freedom would bring down the barbed-wire fences of Bergen-Belsen and of humanity.[8]

THE MUSSAF SERVICE:

ESSENCE OF THE DAY

—II—

The Mussaf service, together with the sounding of the shofar, forms the heart of the Rosh Hashanah prayers. Mussaf is divided into three sections: Kingship (*Malchiyos*), Memories (*Zichronos*), and Shofar (*Shofaros*).

Kingship: Loyalty is the bedrock of any relationship. To be disloyal to a spouse, a friend, or to your country is to shatter the relationship. At this point in the service a Jew must consider where his or her loyalty ultimately lies.

*And everything that was made will know that You made it.
And all that was formed will know who formed it.*

Close your eyes and hear God speaking to you.
"Julie (or whoever you are), your existence in this world is not an accident. I, the creator of the universe—the galaxies and the

vastness of space, the great rain forests and all that fills them, the earth and all the people that have ever inhabited it—I purposely formed, molded and created you.

I made you who you are, placed you in your family, in the time and place of your life. I gave you your strengths and weaknesses.

I ask of you, please, search for your purpose. Strive to allow me into the life I have given you, and know; I will help you."

> **Memories:** Are there things you never forget to do? Push-ups in the morning, returning all your calls at work, telling your children you love them? If you want to know what your priorities truly are on a daily basis, then consider those things you always remember—even without setting the alarm on your watch.

> *You remember everything that has ever occurred…all that is hidden; all that seems to be a secret…A person's innermost thoughts, plans and motivations…You carefully consider everyone's actions…*

It is impossible to fathom God. God is at once above and beyond all that defines and confines us—absolutely transcendent and at the same time imminent. He cares about our every thought and action because he cares about us. We are not asked to fully understand God, only to remember Him and to know that we too are always remembered.

> **Shofar:** Wake up! It's time to rethink and recommit, making sure that we remember where our loyalties lie and never forgetting the commitments we have made.

Repetition of the Mussaf

Unesaneh Tokef / Let Us Relate the Power of the Day

Most prayer books contain a brief account of the story behind this stirring passage, which has become a highlight of the Rosh Hashanah service. It is the story of the great Rabbi Amnon who was slowly dismembered at the orders of a bishop rather than convert and deny his Judaism.

If being Jewish is worth dying for, then it is certainly worth living for.

Teshuva—Tefilah—Tzedakah / Returning—Prayer—Charity

Do you ever feel that life is a juggling act? That you're trying your best to keep the balls in the air while your eyes dart this way and that to see what else may be flying toward you. All the while looking for a job—or a spouse. Raising kids—loving, laughing, and fighting. It isn't easy, is it?

We all have three interwoven spheres of relationships in our lives. I and myself, I and God and I and other human beings. Teshuva is a return to one's true path. To that sense of harmony— even hectic harmony, that flows from expressing your innermost self in the way you live. Prayer is returning to God. Charity is actively expressing our concern for others.

Life is a three-legged pedestal. We struggle for balance.

Adam, Y'sodo May'afar / Man, His Beginning is from Dust

...and his end is dust: He spends the energy of his life to earn his bread; he is like a broken pot, withered grass; a fading flower...

Take pleasure, not pride.

Rabbi Noah Weinberg, <u>48 Ways to Wisdom</u>[9]

Is a rich man any better than a poor man; is a woman who becomes a professor or a doctor any better than a cleaning woman or a cab driver?

When I was a child, school buildings had janitors. Today they have maintenance engineers. The terminology is telling.

There isn't a person in synagogue today who didn't need his diaper changed, and someday, we may find ourselves in that humble position again. If we have the good fortune of wealth, accomplishment or family, then let us be filled with pleasure, not pride.

Atah Zocher / **You Remember**

People say, "I want my children to have the things I never had." Should we not also say, "I want my child to be the person I never was"?

How would you like to be remembered? As someone who was well dressed or someone who was well respected. As a taker or a giver.

We know how we want our children to be remembered, but do we know how they will remember us?

9) I have talents and gifts to share.
10) I want to be a source of joy for others.

YOM KIPPUR

THE TREES

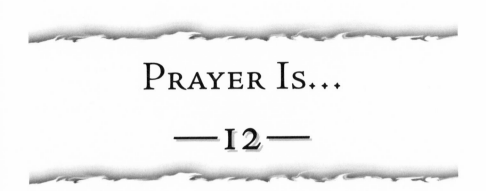

PRAYER IS...

—12—

...A Multifaceted Discipline

Prayer is at once childlike in its simplicity and profound beyond description. But that begs a question.

How can I, having just taken leave of the roaring 80s and now riding the choppy waters of the 1990s, relate to prayer in a meaningful way, in a way that I feel comfortable with. Because to be honest, I do feel that there is something out there—call it God, the Force or whatever you want—and I do want to connect with whatever that something is. I just don't want to be left feeling like some strange religious fanatic in the process.

This chapter contains six perspectives on prayer. Each one presents a different approach to relating to prayer. While these six are by no means exhaustive, I do hope that at least one of them will open a path for you to have a genuine encounter with one of the richest treasures of Jewish life.

In the final analysis, we need to understand that prayer is a highly sophisticated discipline that is not easily mastered. In its fullest sense it demands a lifetime of careful attention and effort. However, there is no doubt that even one sincere moment of prayer is has the potential to be the most moving of experiences.

It is my deepest wish that this chapter will provide you with a thoughtful and sensitive stepping stone into the world of prayer on Rosh Hashanah, on Yom Kippur, and throughout your lifetime.

...Self-inquiry

In Hebrew the most common term for praying is *lehitpalel*. This word, *lehitpalel*, is a reflexive verb that literally means, to examine and judge oneself. The particular objects of our scrutiny are our own attitudes and actions. From this perspective, prayer is a private encounter with ourselves in the presence of God.

It is axiomatic to any process of inquiry and assessment that there must exist some basic standard or criteria against which judgment will be made. For instance, if you take your watch to a jeweler and ask the simple question, "Is this a good watch?" the jeweler can only give a meaningful reply if he has a standard of quality and craftsmanship against which to judge your watch. At one end of his scale is a ten-dollar "throw-away" watch and at the other extreme is a top-of-the-line Rolex. The issue is, where on this continuum does your watch fit in?

This approach to prayer uses the words and concepts embodied in the prayer book as "top-of-the-line" standards against which we hold up our own feelings, attitudes and actions. We reflect on where we fit in, ponder why we rate ourselves the way we do, seriously consider our actions and think about how we can improve.

In life it is essential to know "where you stand." Be it on the job, in a relationship, or on a particular social or political issue. In Jewish life you must also know where you stand. If we read in the daily prayer book the words, *sound the great shofar for our freedom, raise a banner to gather our exiles and speedily gather us together from the four corners of the earth to our land*, then we have to ask ourselves: (a) In addition to sending my checks to various worthy causes, am I really bothered by the fact that there are Jews in Syria or Yemen who are unable to emigrate to Israel? and, (b) If you are, how bothered? Have I ever cried at the thought of a Jewish mother whose husband languishes in prison for no reason? And if we read the words, *Vekabtzenu* (and gather us) *L'artzenu* (to our land), do I really think of Israel as my home? Would I be proud of my children if they chose to settle there? Do I in any way long for the Jewish people to be united again in Jerusalem?

These are not easy or comfortable questions, but then again self-assessment is never easy. In order to grow you must first know where you stand. When using this approach to prayer I suggest you choose one or two concepts to focus on each time you pray. You can either decide ahead of time which concepts they will be, or you can choose them as the prayer service progresses. In either case the idea is quality and not quantity. One concept is certainly sufficient if you earnestly reflect on it. This approach can open up a whole world of self-discovery as well as personal, spiritual, and Jewish growth.

...An Instrument for Change

There is a question that students of Jewish thought have been asking for centuries. The question is this: "If (as Judaism claims) whatever God does for us is exactly what is best for us, then why do we ever ask for anything in our prayers? Isn't what we already have precisely what we need?"

The approach to dealing with this question is quite telling in terms of the Jewish view of what human beings should be doing with their lives. (This question also raises other sensitive issues, but for now we will deal only with how it relates to prayer.) Judaism sees life as a steady stream of opportunities for learning, growing, and changing. This conscious engagement of those opportunities is known as *tikkun ha-middot*, or the constant refinement of human character and deed that comes through ever-increasing self-awareness. In the vernacular we call it "working on yourself."

The answer to our original question stems from this slice of Jewish *Weltanschauung* and is as follows: If I grow and change throughout the course of my life; if in terms of my attitudes, inclinations and actions I transcend my former self, then what is best for me will also change. In other words, prayer itself is an experiential medium for effecting personal growth. Therefore, the fact that I can make requests during prayer tells me that I ought to be a different person after prayer than when I began. What was best for me when I began my prayers is not necessarily what is best for me when I have finished.

If this is so, then there is a follow-up question that must also be asked. How is it that prayer can effect personal growth and change?

Consider if you will the annual phenomenon of New Year's resolutions. I would like to suggest that the reason these resolutions rarely last is not because they were unrealistic or because unforeseen obstacles arose, but rather because the initial commitment was only half-hearted. And a half-hearted commitment is no commitment at all.

Our sages teach us that "all beginnings are difficult." The first step to achieving anything meaningful in life is the commitment to do so. It is the lack of a full commitment that will usually present itself as the most daunting obstacle on your desired path. If your commitment is resolute then you have already overcome your greatest obstacle to success. The rest is all but guaranteed.

As we read and take to heart the values and ideals expressed in the language of the prayers, we must always ask ourselves: Do I really mean what I am saying? Am I truly committed to the values I am now uttering, or is this just lip service?

The opportunity is growth, the essential ingredient is commitment, and the means is prayer.*

---

* Keep in mind that in prayer we are having a personal encounter with God. He knows if we mean what we say or not, so don't kid yourself. If you don't mean it then don't commit. But if you do, then commit all the way.

...Talking to God

Four out of five people in America say that God answers their prayers. What about you? Have you ever prayed and really meant it? Have you ever spoken to God or cried out to Him from the depths of your being? Did He answer you?

$E=MC^2$ is a relatively simple equation. It is also one of the most penetrating notions to ever occupy the human mind. Prayer is also quite simple. God is here and you can speak to Him. That's all there is to it. No tricks, no intermediaries, just talk. Is there anything more simple or anything more magnificent?

God is the designer and creator of the universe, the source of all existence: the stars that blanket the sky, the stately snowcapped peaks and the waves crashing on the rocky coast. All of this and more. And all of creation pales to nothingness in the face of its creator. This creator. This God. You can speak to Him. At this very moment you are in His presence. You can learn to feel that. To sense his presence. You can touch the ultimate.

But there is a part of us that is afraid. "What if I speak to Him and I *do* feel a presence. Then what will happen to me?" Or perhaps you just feel sort of, well, weird; awkwardly out of place. That all makes sense. Look, you're not used to this. Don't worry though, God won't bite you. Like anything else prayer will take practice and patience, but in the end there is nothing more sublime than speaking to God.

O nce there was a king whose son wanted to go out into the world. He wanted to travel, to explore and to make it on his own. After some time he found that he was desperately short of cash and that his credit cards had all expired. He was far, far away from his father's kingdom, in a land whose ways and language were very different from his own. Many years passed and he became a successful and respected citizen in his new country. One day, a feeling overcame him. He wanted to go home, to see his father again.

> *And so he began another long journey. After many months he was again on the soil of his father's kingdom. It was a land whose ways and tongue he had forgotten. There he stood at the entrance to the palace. Alone. Unable to communicate or to identify himself. He was home but he was still so very lost. From beneath a window to his father's chamber he desperately cried out in his foreign tongue—faa-ther, faa-ther! So many lost years flashed through his mind. His voice cracked in helplessness. Inside the chamber the king heard a frightful cry. He did not know the language, but that voice—even after so long, he knew the voice of his son.*
>
> *They wept as they embraced. Welcome home son, welcome home.*

God is waiting to hear our voices. The words and the language really don't matter. What matters is hearing the voice of a child. We can talk to Him. Even if it's just a few whispered words. "God, I'm home." Don't worry, it's okay. Tell God that you feel a little uncomfortable but that you really do want to feel close. Tell Him that you know He's there, you know He's listening and you want to come home.

It may take a while, but eventually you will see. There is nothing as simple, or as uplifting, as being home.

...Your Inner Life

The worst thing about the proverbial glass house is not its susceptibility to stones, but rather its dramatic lack of privacy.

I know a woman who is a psychologist working with prisoners in a state-run maximum-security facility. She tells me that in prison there is a horrific lack of privacy. Even in the bathroom there are no walls around you or doors to close. Just a dank room full of cold steel toilets where other men sit and stare at you. This, she says, breeds a terrible rage that tears at every prisoner's soul.

We all lead two lives and live in two worlds: an outer life and an inner life, one public and one private.

After the bank teller says "Good morning" and asks how she can help, how do you respond? Is it with a prerecorded "I'm fine thanks, how are you?" only then to drone on about the transactions you would like to execute? Or even in the midst of a world where people deal with one another like so many PINs, do you respond to this person as a person?

It is essential that there be a part of your life that is secluded and private. Not an external hiding place, but a chamber within your heart; an internal study to which you can retreat, to contemplate, to talk to God or just to hear yourself breathe.

Rabbi Shlomo Volbe, possessor of the type of ennobled heart and mind that is unique to the holy city of Jerusalem, describes prayer as "sudden quietness." Prayer is a rite of visitation to a very private place in your heart; and it is from there that your equilibrium will flow. In prayer we take the ideas expressed in our words and thoughtfully meditate on them. We try to understand them and to feel them, to let them permeate our being and become a part of who we are. Prayer is the guarantor of our inner lives. The moments we spend in prayer allow us to take quiet refuge from the dissonance of our outer life and reacquaint ourselves with a peaceful inner core. Prayer is that which preserves and nourishes the indispensable private domain of heart and soul. Without that privacy, if we never encounter a self other than our outer self, if we never live other than in full view of the world, then we can easily slide into a silent rage—or more likely, shrivel up and die.

...Being Connected to the Jewish People

Did you ever notice that the bulk of our prayers, in fact the entire *Amidah*, are in the plural? Help *us*, rescue *us*, return *us*, and so on.

I remember being in Paris with a backpack on my back and a *kippa* on my head. I was not quite twenty-one and I was engaged in that hallowed rite of passage known as looking for oneself, as if some spiritual clone of every young American lives in a quaint loft somewhere in Europe.

The most phenomenal thing happened to me in Paris. Wherever I went I was besieged by a curious mix of Parisian Jews. None of them looked particularly Jewish, they just sort of stepped out from the sea of faces that filled the avenues of Paris.

"Would you like to come to my house for dinner?" one of them asked.

"Do you need a place to sleep?" inquired another.

"Can I help you?" "Do you need directions?" "Take my phone number in case you need anything." I was even offered money!

All of this from Jews to whom I was a complete stranger. But there I was, like so many others, roaming the streets of Paris and thinking about life. There was only one difference: the *kippa* on my head. And thus, we were one—one people and one family, inexorably bound together.

And so when we pray we do so in the plural. Because each one of us possesses an identity that reaches for beyond our individual selves. We are each a living cell in a body that is three thousand years young. We pray in the plural because we exist in our fellow Jews, as they exist in us.

...Tuning into the Cosmos

A carpenter uses a hammer and nails, a writer his ink and quill, but what does God use when He wants to fashion a universe? There is a fantastically expressive Jewish idea that says that the tools God used for creation were the very letters of the Hebrew alphabet. In fact, the first things God created were the letters, and then He used them to construct the rest of existence.

The Hebrew language is a multi-layered superstructure containing limitless nuances, each reflecting a different dimension of insight. Each Hebrew letter has numerous levels of meaning. Let us use the letter *aleph*, the first letter in the alphabet, as an archetype.

1) The numerical value of the letter.

The *aleph*, because it is the first letter in the alphabet, has a numerical value of one. It follows that *beit*, the second letter, would have a numerical value of two and so on throughout the alphabet. God, as the Jewish people taught the world, is One.

2) The global concept represented by the letter.

Every Hebrew letter is also a word and thus incorporates the concept that the word expresses. The word *aleph* expresses the concept of leadership or to champion. A military commander is an *aluf*.

3) The proto-concept of the letter.

The Talmud teaches that each letter contains an idea related to the first time the letter appears in the Torah as the first letter of a word. The first time *aleph* appears as the first letter of a word is in the word *elohim*, which is one of God's names. Therefore, the *aleph* signifies an aspect of Godliness.

4) The form of the letter.

The letter *aleph*, when written in a Torah scroll, is actually a composite of two *yuds* and a *vav*. The letter *yud* represents the unity of God and has the numerical value of ten. The *vav*, in Hebrew, serves as a grammatical link: *vav* as a prefix means "and," thus connecting two thoughts. *Vav* has the numerical value of six.

❀ The letter *aleph* is written with one *yud* above the *vav* and the other *yud* below it. Thus what we have in the letter *aleph* are two expressions of the *yud*, an upper *yud* and a lower *yud*.

Aleph (the leader) and *aleph* (the embodiment of unity and divinity) are embodied in a form that portrays God's unity in sovereignty. The God of the heavenly, spiritual sphere (the upper *yud*) is the same as the God below in the earthly realm (the lower *yud*).

❋ In the Torah different "names" are used for God, each representing a different aspect of how God relates to the world. The primary name for God contains such deep spirituality that it is ineffable; it is too sacred to be pronounced. Looking again at the letter *aleph*, we find that the numerical value of two *yuds* (10 + 10) plus *vav* (6) is twenty-six. Twenty-six is also the numerical value of the ineffable name of God.

The Hebrew letters and words are far more than symbolic images and sounds. Each letter is a living organism. These primordial letters of creation gave birth to the totality of existence. Contained within each letter are not only hidden meanings but hidden capabilities as well.

The early sages who composed our prayers held within their minds and souls the keys with which to unlock the creative forces concealed in the Hebrew language.

When we speak, we create. We create impressions, feelings, ideas and even revolutions; simply through the force of our words. On a much deeper level, the authors of our prayers knew how to use the letters and words in such a way that they would work to attune our souls and connect us to Godliness. Beyond the manifest meaning of the words lies a coded message, a spiritual software package that works to direct and connect our souls in ways we are unaware.

Prayer, particularly in Hebrew, has the capacity to help us touch and be affected by a spiritual reality that is far beyond the purview of our ordinary means of comprehension.*

---

* Judaism is clear in its assertion that a person can pray in any language. However, there are dimensions of the prayer experience that can never survive a translation from Hebrew. A recommended starting point for one who hopes to eventually pray in Hebrew is to begin by learning and even memorizing the first paragraph of the *Shema*, as well as the first paragraph of the *Amidah*.

KOL NIDRE: THE CREDIBILITY FACTOR

—13—

One winter morning my wife noticed that a small envelope had been dropped by our back door. It had no name, no address, nothing. Inside was a thank-you note. A few words had been written in haste with a signature that was barely legible.

Our backyard serves as an occasional shortcut or meeting place for some of our neighbors. We're new on the block and it seems we are centrally located in the midst of some old neighborhood friends.

My wife tacked the card to the bulletin board in our hallway. In a day or two she would ask the neighbors if it was theirs. Weeks and months passed as did the long winter nights. As for the card, it got lost on that bulletin board, covered by a sea of coupons and school notices.

Autumn is beautiful where we live. The streets, particularly ours, are ablaze with colors: fiery reds, oranges and yellows of every shade. One day there was a knock on the door. It was that man everyone sees but no one knows. You see him all over town riding a wobbly, rusted bicycle laden with old bags and rags full of God knows what—probably more bags and rags. The elements don't seen to faze him; he just keeps on peddling.

"Would you like me to rake your leaves?" he asked. Sure I said, why not. At least he has enough self-respect to try to earn some money. Besides, he had once shoveled the snow from our driveway and did a pretty good job. My wife cautioned, though, "let's keep the girls inside while he's working out there. These days, sadly, you just never know."

Autumn passed, as did Succos and Chanukah. Before we knew it the snows had returned. Winter too has a beauty all its own and we were blessed with one of those storms that blankets a city with early morning silence.

The girls and I were outside building snowmen, one for each child. A big one for our five year old, a smaller one for our two and a half year old and a tiny one for the baby. "Excuse me sir," came the voice of the man on the bicycle, "would you like me to shovel your drive?" Why not, I thought. It will help the guy out, not to mention myself. He was shoveling and we were having the time of our lives. My two and a half year old, as friendly and curious as can be, asked him, "What's your name?" "J.D.," he replied, "what's yours?"

Later, as we were putting the final touches on our snowkids, my daughter said, "Abba, I love J.D., he's a nice man." "He sure is," I said, and we went inside to warm up and have some lunch.

Back in the house my wife had made a couple of sandwiches to give to the man on the bicycle when he finished his work. "Mommy," the little one said, "I love J.D." "That's

> nice," she said, but neither of us wanted her to feel too good about this nice, but curious stranger.
>
> A week or so later, after J.D. had shoveled our drive for the second time that winter, my wife found herself doing one of the tasks she had been postponing for months: clearing off the bulletin board in the hall. Away with old school notices and expired coupons—up with a new schedule of community lectures. She put aside that faceless thank-you card. It will be embarrassing, she thought, but I'll ask the neighbors if it's theirs anyway.
>
> The card fell open on the table and she read it. "Thank you for your help and your kindness," signed, "J.D."

We still haven't gotten over that thank-you card. That first winter when the man on the bicycle had shoveled our drive we didn't even know his name. I paid him nicely and my wife gave him a container of chicken that was left over from Shabbos. He reluctantly took the chicken—he still had his pride—thanked us for the work and wobbled off on his overloaded bicycle through the snowy streets.

Who is he? Where does he live? Does he have a family? One thing I do know, he went to a lot of effort just to buy a thank-you note and return to our house to drop it at our back door.

Says a lot about "J.D."—doesn't it?

          ~   ~   ~

It's hard to be forgiving. Throughout the course of the year, in one way or another, people hurt us; emotionally, physically, monetarily. In the vast majority of instances the hurt passes, leaving few if any enduring marks. Or we may realize it was actually our honor—our ego—that was more bruised than anything else. Yet it is still hard to forgive.

What about you? Did you hurt anyone this year—knowingly or perhaps without even realizing it at the time? We're human. How can it be that we don't step on a few toes or overlook a few sentiments, a few feelings that others hold dear? It's so hard to forgive, but it's nothing like asking for forgiveness. We so want to be perfect, and to say "I'm sorry" is to dredge up a thousand shortcomings. It can be so humbling, so very unappealing.

The Tefilah Zakkah is an often overlooked little prayer said just before Kol Nidre on Yom Kippur Eve. There we are in synagogue, we're late, we're exchanging New Year's greetings or checking out the latest style in ties or dresses. We just don't have time for Tefilah Zakkah, after all, doesn't Yom Kippur really begin with Kol Nidre anyway?

Tefilah Zakkah contains one of the most important prayers we will say throughout the entire Yom Kippur service. Quite simply it is a paragraph that says, "since I know that there is no righteous person in the world who does not sin against his fellow man, either monetarily or physically, in deed or in speech, therefore my heart aches within me... May no person be punished on my account. And just like I forgive everyone so may you grant me favor in every person's eyes that they may also grant me full forgiveness."

Sure, we hurt people during the year, but that's not representative of who we are. We don't want to be a source of pain or hardship in someone else's life. In a few instances we may have said we're sorry, but most times we just gloss them over. We hope and pray that people will forgive us, that they will look beyond the surface and know that in truth there is much more to who we are than the moment of pain we inflicted. And we too must try to look beyond the surface, to know that each person is a world—complex and confounding; to themselves as well as others.

Tefilah Zakkah can bring us so close. To others and to ourselves as well. Isn't that how Yom Kippur should really begin?

Kol Nidre

If you vowed to do something this year and now realize that you cannot live up to your word; this is Kol Nidre.

There are probably more Jews in synagogue for Kol Nidre than at any other time during the year. The question is, why? What is it about Kol Nidre that keeps the crowds coming back?

Could it possibly be that consciously or unconsciously every Jew senses that Kol Nidre touches the most sensitive nerve of their humanity? That without Kol Nidre you can't have a Yom Kippur? That without Kol Nidre you can't have a life.

In Kol Nidre we make this statement: I realize that if I have made any verbal commitments, if I gave my word on anything, then without recourse to some higher authority there is no backing out. My word is my word—period. My word locks into place a reality that I can no longer undo. That reality, that word, binds me.

Imagine a world where contracts didn't have to be signed. Where a person's word was "as good as gold" and a handshake was a done deal. Imagine if people actually lived with that kind of trust in one another. Imagine the integrity.

Beyond the elimination of mountains of paperwork and half the legal profession, it would be a different world. There is no other way to describe it. An entirely different world.

Kol Nidre is a time when we take a searing look inside. We ask ourselves, who can count on my word? Can my children, or my spouse, my friends, my boss? Can God? Can I! Can I count on my own word; Do I trust myself?

Without credibility we have nothing. With it we have everything. Thus, Kol Nidre.

11) *God, please show me how to be close to you.*
12) *I will not lose sight of who and what is most important to me.*

Teshuva: Four Steps

To Greatness

—14—

*M*y *brother was fifteen when he bought his first horse. Unlike other kids who rode bicycles, skateboards, or motorcycles, my brother preferred a horse. Now this was no ordinary horse. This was an imposing jet black thoroughbred named Seriously, a retired race horse.*

I took my brother up on his offer and decided to take Seriously for a ride around the neighborhood, a ride that was almost my last. Not far from my parents' home was a long, wide boulevard that featured expansive grassy islands running down the middle of the road. On one side of these islands traffic flowed in one direction and on the other side it moved in the opposite direction. In between each island was a crossover point so that cars could cut through and change direction. It was one of those crossover points that was almost my doom.

When old Seriously reached the top of that long open stretch of grass he had a sudden flash of déjà vu. He was once again a young, virile thoroughbred poised at the starting gate ready to impress the world with his speed and power. And there sat I, the unsuspecting victim of this wishful leap back to the days of one horse's youth.

A bloodcurdling scream was lodged in my throat and Seriously was off to the races. The harder I pulled on the reins and the more violently I kicked his ribs, the less he paid attention to me. Faster and faster he galloped. We were closing in on one of those crossover points and it was clear that the horse had absolutely no intention of stopping to look both ways before crossing. Through the horrified tears in my eyes I could see that a red Cadillac and a new Mercedes sports car were both using the crossover and were totally oblivious to the horse and rider headed their way. At least, I thought, I'd go out in style.

To make a long story short, I survived, though I don't think I've mounted a horse since.

Today, my brother lives on a farm with his wife and baby, raises chickens, owns a goat named Blackey and still rides his horse whenever he gets a chance. What's amazing to me is that he can ride bareback and has no need for reins. He just jumps up and is instantly one with the animal. It responds to his commands and takes him—with more grace and power than my brother could ever muster—wherever he wants to go. He is the picture of a rider in perfect control of his horse. And me, well, I already told you that story.

Body and Soul: Want Versus Feel

When our sages wanted to find an image that would capture the internal dynamics of human life, they chose a horse and rider. This is their picture of man and of the human condition.

There is a basic tension in life that we all feel. This is the tension that exists between what we want to do and what we feel like doing. Does this sound familiar? Do you recognize the tension? It works like this: I want to help my son with his homework—I feel like relaxing in front of the television. I want to lose fifteen pounds—I feel like having a piece of cheesecake. I want to visit my parents—I feel like playing tennis. I want to make a difference with my life—I feel like just getting by and minding my own business. I want to achieve the greatness of my potential—I feel like settling for being average.

The rider, what we want to do, is our soul. The horse, what we feel like doing, is our body. Mind you, Judaism never denigrates the body or physical pleasures. Quite the opposite. Judaism says that the pleasures of the physical world are here to be enjoyed, to be fully partaken of. There is just one question: who is in control? Is this a skilled rider leading a faithful obedient horse, or is this a rider who has lost control and is at the mercy of his horse's every whim and desire?

The Mistakes We Make

We all make mistakes. Almost everyday we do things that we really don't want to be doing. It's a fascinating phenomenon.

When was the last time you had the following experience? You were confronted with the opportunity to do something that you perceived as being wrong, something you clearly did not want to do; but a funny thing happened on the way to Yom Kippur. The very act that you didn't want to do, you did anyway. Fascinating. Before you did it, you knew it was a mistake and you didn't want to do it. While you were doing it, you knew it was a mistake and you didn't want to be doing it, and after the fact you looked back in wonderment. Not feeling very good about yourself, you pondered, "Why did I do that?"

The answer is this: We are all geniuses, every one of us. When it comes to our ability to rationalize, the Einstein in all of us begins to surface. We are capable of the most convincing bits of intellectual dexterity, temporarily tying our minds in one convoluted knot after another, thereby enabling ourselves to do what we feel like doing instead of what we really want to do.

This is the root of many of the mistakes we make in life. We all want to do what's right. Only sometimes we rationalize and do what we feel like doing instead.

Defining Our Terms

One of the most common words in your prayer book is "sin." It's not a very pleasant sounding word. Certainly no one wants to look at himself or herself as a sinner. In Hebrew, the generic term for sin is *chet*. This term literally means "to make a mistake." Sins, no thanks. But mistakes—sure—we all make mistakes.

The issue on Yom Kippur is this: How do we correct the mistakes of our past and avoid repeating them in the future? If we can understand this, then we possess the key to unlocking an enormous reservoir of latent potential for greatness that would otherwise lie dormant.

This is *teshuva*. The common translation of *teshuva* is "repentance." Again, a rather foreign sounding idea. The proper translation of the word *teshuva* is "to return." *Teshuva* is an animated technique for locating the rationalizations that lie at the root of our mistakes: recognizing them, dealing with them and eliminating them.

Four Steps to *Teshuva*—Four Steps to Greatness

1) Regret (*charata*)
Regret, as opposed to guilt, is that state of vexation in which one feels a sense of loss. If you misplace your wallet with a thousand dollars in it, you feel regret, not guilt. You have lost something of value.

In our striving for growth we must first see that our mistakes in life have resulted in the loss of something we deem to be dear and important.

2) **Abandonment** (*aziva*)

As General Schwarzkopf once put it, "Gentleman, all I can say is we identified the target in question and it no longer exists." Rationalization is the enemy and *aziva* is an internal mission of search and destroy.

I lost my wallet, or worse yet, I lost a friend; now how do I avoid repeating the same mistake? Once you feel the loss it's then time to set out on a personal mission of search and destroy. You must identify the rationalization, see what it was that enticed you into that cerebral snare and understand the basic untruth that is the nucleus of rationalization.

Now you must issue a cease and desist order. Stop the rationalization and put a halt to the action it sanctioned.

3) **Confession** (*vidduy*)

In other words, "Now go and say you're sorry." There is perhaps no greater torture in a child's mind than being told he has to apologize. Stick bamboo shoots under my nails, tie me to the rack—anything—but don't make me say I'm sorry!

Because when you verbalize your regret it makes everything all too real, like being on a darkened stage with the spotlight on you. There is no escape. The truth about your actions and their hurtful consequences are laid bare for all to see when you utter those simple words: "I'm sorry. I feel awful about what I did, it won't happen again. I promise."

4) **Resolve** (*kabalah*)

Say what you mean, "I'm sorry," and mean what you say, "It won't happen again." With this final act of commitment never to repeat the same mistake, you have come full circle. You have returned.

If a friend comes to you and you see that she sincerely regrets what she did, understands her mistake, wishes it had never happened and with a heavy heart apologizes and pledges never to repeat it, would you not be immediately forgiving?

What if that friend was your daughter, or what if that daughter was you?

Keeping Your Eye on the Ball

Teshuva is challenging. As a matter of fact, it can be a very uncomfortable challenge. It can be hard, and humbling, to admit our mistakes. Then to actually make changes certainly takes a lot of work and effort. What we need to remember is that growth and change are also a pleasure.

There seems to be a part of us that is all too ready to avoid work, effort and discomfort. The key to *teshuva*, to lasting growth, is to eliminate the confusion of comfort with pleasure. Comfort is nothing more than the absence of pain; while pain and effort and discomfort are usually prerequisites for lasting pleasure.

Think about it: Haven't your most meaningful, lasting accomplishments and deepest experiences of pleasure come at the price of great and often uncomfortable efforts? It's one of those regrettable facts of life. Picture two men at the top of a mountain: one who climbed and one who was dropped there by a helicopter. The guy who climbed will derive far more pleasure from his experience of the summit because he climbed to the top instead of taking the comfortable route.

So what can we do to overcome our tendency to flee from the necessary discomfort that is a part of *teshuva* and growth? We can stay focused and keep our eye on the ball—the ball of pleasure. The pleasure of growth, of moving ahead and of accessing more and more of our potential.

It actually hurts more when I'm at home than when I'm playing. It's like when I'm focused on the game, the pain goes away.

Brady Anderson, Baltimore Orioles[10]

13) I am able to forgive, to mend and to move forward.
14) Everyone has problems; I will find ways to manage and to progress.

Practical Application

One of the pitfalls inherent in Yom Kippur is "biting off more than you can chew." I would therefore like to offer some practical suggestions:

1) Look at your life in terms of three spheres of relationships: one with yourself, one with God, and one with other people. Then, make a list of five mistakes you have made in each sphere and rank them from most to least serious.

2) Take your list with you to synagogue on Yom Kippur and plan a strategy for the day. For example: On Yom Kippur night you will take one of your top three mistakes through the four-step *teshuva* process.* During the morning service, you will concentrate on the next two, and so on. Pacing yourself will make this process easier. And if you don't make it through your whole list this year, there is always next year.

3) Keep your list of mistakes in a private place, but make sure you won't lose track of it. You should try to review this list for fifteen minutes once a month.

4) Remember that *teshuva* is a unique *mitzva*. With other *mitzvot* (commandments) if you are lacking part of the *mitzva*, you lack the whole thing. An *esrog* and a *lulav* are made up of four species, but if you are missing one, it is as if you have nothing. With regard to *teshuva*, every effort you make and every step you take brings you closer to where you want to be. No one can ever take away a step of progress, a step of growth or a step toward greatness.

---

* Regarding mistakes where you have hurt or wronged another person, it is most appropriate to ask that person for forgiveness before Yom Kippur.

MOMENTUM BUILDER

—15—

Football is a game of momentum.

NFL sportscaster

A person should always study what his heart desires.

Talmud

No college professor ever told her students to study whatever their hearts desired. Just the opposite. The best way to master any body of knowledge is to pursue a well thought out course of study that proceeds logically from one step to the next. Why then, when it comes to the vast sea of Jewish wisdom—the Torah, Talmud, Maimonides, Kabbalah and all the rest—do our sages tell us to study whatever our little hearts desire?

The answer is momentum.

In the pursuit of Jewish knowledge and wisdom, the best place to start is with whatever brings you a sense of satisfaction and accomplishment. Achieving a sense of satisfaction and accomplishment enables you to create a wave of momentum that will then carry you on to the great challenge, the vast sea, of Jewish learning.

The same principle holds true when it comes to personal growth, to spiritual advancement and to change. One needs to create a positive wave of momentum. This is done by choosing one aspect of your life that you want to enhance, an aspect that you think is readily achievable and that when completed will give you great satisfaction, and beginning there.

MOMENTUM BUILDER™ 1.0

The following exercise—MOMENTUM BUILDER™—is designed to help you identify areas for growth in your life that have the potential to serve as catalysts for further growth. Personal growth, refining or changing aspects of how we live, polishing our character, enhancing our relationships and elevating the spiritual dimension of our lives, is always a challenge—sometimes a daunting challenge. The Momentum Builder exercise will help you manage the challenge of growth by identifying Momentum Builders: achievable first steps to take along the path of growth. Think of these steps as a way to make resolutions you can actually keep.

Momentum Builder will enable you to do four things:

1) To identify areas of potential growth.

2) To assess how much effort will be required to grow in each area.

3) To determine how much satisfaction you will derive from successful growth in that dimension of your life.

4) To start building momentum in your personal growth.

MOMENTUM BUILDER: EASY AS A-B-C

You will be presented with a list of statements and will be asked to score those statements in three different ways. The three scores will be as follows:

(A) SELF-EVALUATION.

On a scale of one to five, how do you feel about yourself in terms of the statement being made? (1= Disappointed. I'm not very happy with this aspect of my life. 5= Terrific. I feel very good about this aspect of my life.)

(B) PROJECTED EFFORT REQUIRED.

On a scale of one to five, how much effort will it take for me to grow in this area of my life? (1= Ugh. It will take more energy than I have to master this part of my life. 5= No sweat. I can easily accomplish this.)

(C) SATISFACTION FACTOR.

On a scale of one to five, how much pleasure and satisfaction will I derive if I am able to achieve significant growth in this area? (1= Not much. I would not feel substantially different if I grew in this area. 5= Wow! What an incredible feeling if I could achieve a breakthrough in this area.)

A SAMPLE STATEMENT & SCORES

STATEMENT: I am the type of person that others feel they can turn to if they need help.

SCORES: (A) SELF-EVALUATION   3
                 (B) PROJECTED EFFORT REQUIRED   4
                 (C) SATISFACTION FACTOR   4

ANALYSIS OF SCORES

(A) SELF-EVALUATION. The score of three indicates that this is an area in which I would like to grow.

(B) PROJECTED EFFORT REQUIRED. The score of four indicates that it is realistic for me to consider trying to grow in this area.

(C) SATISFACTION FACTOR. The score of four indicates that I would feel much better about myself if I could grow in this area of my life.

MOMENTUM INDEX

The ideal candidates for generating momentum—known as Momentum Builders—will be those statements that have a SELF-EVALUATION score of two or three, a PROJECTED EFFORT REQUIRED score of three or four and a SATISFACTION FACTOR score of three, four or five. (See sample statement and scores above.)

PLANS OF ACTION

For all those statements that qualify as potential Momentum Builders, you will need to write a short plan of action. This plan will describe what you need to do that will enable you to grow in the way you would like. Your plan of action should be short, specific and realistic in the context of your daily life.

SAMPLE PLANS OF ACTION

I. To become more of *the type of person that others feel they can turn to if they need help,* I plan to: Once a month, think about the people I know (family, friends and colleagues) and ask myself if there is anything I am aware of that they need help with in their lives. The help can be large or small, but whatever it may be, I'm going to either try to help or find a way to get them the help they need.

II. To become more *patient with other people's shortcomings,* I plan to: Make a list of three people who have shortcomings that get on my nerves and then write down one or two qualities that make that person likable or beautiful. Additionally I will ask myself, "What quality does this person possess that I can learn from?" Finally, I will list one or two of my own shortcomings that may annoy other people.

BUILDING MOMENTUM

After using the Momentum Builder exercise, and after devising a few plans of action, the next step is to choose the plan of action that you feel offers the highest likelihood of success. This plan will be your optimal Momentum Builder—your first step toward building momentum for personal growth.

The following is a sample list of statements to be used with MOMENTUM BUILDER™. (Feel free to adapt any of these statements to fit your life better and to add new statements of your own.)

1) I have the courage to take a stand when I see injustice.
(A) SELF-EVALUATION ___
(B) PROJECTED EFFORT REQUIRED ___
(C) SATISFACTION FACTOR ___
PLAN OF ACTION:

2) I appreciate the blessings in my life.
(A) SELF-EVALUATION ___
(B) PROJECTED EFFORT REQUIRED ___
(C) SATISFACTION FACTOR ___
PLAN OF ACTION:

3) When my children (or friends, spouse, etc.) speak to me, I give them my full attention.
(A) SELF-EVALUATION ___
(B) PROJECTED EFFORT REQUIRED ___
(C) SATISFACTION FACTOR ___
PLAN OF ACTION:

4) My customers and clients feel that they can trust me.
(A) SELF-EVALUATION ___
(B) PROJECTED EFFORT REQUIRED ___
(C) SATISFACTION FACTOR ___
PLAN OF ACTION:

5) I don't let it bother me when things don't work out the way I planned.
(A) SELF-EVALUATION ___
(B) PROJECTED EFFORT REQUIRED ___
(C) SATISFACTION FACTOR ___
PLAN OF ACTION:

6) I let my spouse know that he or she is far more important to me than my business or career.
7) I possess adequate knowledge of my Jewish heritage.
8) I greet people cheerfully.
9) Spirituality is a regular part of my life.
10) I contribute to my community.
11) I try to help the Jewish people.
12) My parents know how much I appreciate all they have done for me.
13) I carefully think through important decisions.
14) I am a kind and giving person.
15) Personal growth is one of my highest priorities.
16) I don't speak negatively about others.
17) I look for the good in other people.
18) I think about how God would want me to live.
19) I am a person who seeks knowledge and wisdom.
20) I make time for those I love.
21) I am patient with other people's shortcomings.
22) To me, success is a state of mind.
23) I enjoy and appreciate life's simple pleasures.
24) I keep my word.

25) I introspect, think about my life and strive to improve where I can.

26) I respect people because of who they are, not because of what they have.

27) When I make a mistake, I can admit it.

28) I try to be proactive and to create my path in life, not just do what everyone else is doing.

29) I keep in touch with old friends.

30) I think about the values and ideals I want my children to have.

31) I feel that life is a gift to be cherished.

32) I am doing my best to pass Judaism on to the next generation.

33) I'm not too proud to ask for help.

34) If my friends are doing something I don't think is right, I'm not afraid to tell them, or at least I choose not to join them.

35) I am sensitive to other people's feelings.

36) I look for opportunities to help people.

37) When I have a responsibility, I follow through.

38) I take time for myself.

39) I listen to my soul.

40) I search for meaning.

41) I have confidence in my ability to make good decisions.

42) I have good self-control.

43) I am aware of my strengths and my weaknesses.

44) I do the best I can and leave success and failure to God.

45) I welcome constructive criticism.

46) I look for ways to give pleasure to my spouse.

47) I try to be enthusiastic, at least once a day.

48) I am honest in my romantic relationships.

49) I don't take friendships for granted.

I truly hope you find the Momentum Builder exercise to be beneficial. I want to applaud any effort you make using it and, at the same time, if it's just not for you, that's okay. I'm sure you will find many other useful techniques for growth within these holidays.

Highlights of the Yom Kippur Morning Service

—16—

Birchas HaShachar—Morning Blessings

Asher Yatzar / Who Has Designed Man with Wisdom

I have a friend, and anyone who knows him will tell you he's driven. The man simply operates at a different level of intensity than you or I. So I asked, "What happened? What is it that lights your fire ?"

This is the story he told me:

> *I was in high school and my parents were going away for the weekend. "Michael," my father asked, "do me a favor and finish painting the garage this weekend." I agreed.*

> *Not long after my parents pulled out of the driveway did another car with three of my friends pull in. "But Mike, you know how beautiful the woods are this time of year..." It wasn't an easy decision, but I opted out.*
>
> *Later that evening I was informed that my friends had all died in a horrible collision. I was a survivor, still am; driven for the rest of my life. Because I know. I know I've got a mission.*

We are all survivors. And as long as we possess the gift we call life, we have a mission.

Think about who you are: your unique circumstance in life, your strengths, weaknesses and special abilities. For ourselves and for our families. For the Jewish people and for all humankind. We all have a mission.

Birchas HaTorah / Blessings for the Torah

There are 613 commandments in the Torah. Among them are love your neighbor as yourself, do not murder, and love God.

The Talmud states that if you could put 612 commandments on one side of a scale and just 1 commandment on the other, that there is 1 commandment that would outweigh all the rest.

And just what is this most weighty of all commandments? It is the commandment to study the wisdom of the Torah. How many things can you think of that are more essential than acquiring wisdom—the wisdom necessary to build a close and loving marriage, to raise children, to maintain friendships and to get the most out of life.

To pursue wisdom, understanding and insight is the ultimate commandment.

Pesukei D'Zimrah—Verses of Song

Hallu Es Hashem / Praise God from the Heavens

Our sages say, *"there is no artist like our God."*
We know that; just look around.

Which is more beautiful, the tree in front of your home or the painting of a tree in a gallery? As wondrous as a painting may be, it remains a mere approximation of reality. Yet we think nothing of a group of people staring wide-eyed at a painting in a gallery; however, put that same group of people in front of a tree on your lawn and you will immediately dial 911 for help.

The painting is a reminder. No, it's a window. It calls our attention to the infinite beauty of a tree. The tree too is a window. Step through, for the infinite lies beyond.

Yishtabach / May Your Name Be Praised

This is the closing prayer in the *Pesukei D'Zimrah*, the preparatory portion of the morning prayer service.

There are fifteen expressions of praises to God in this paragraph. In the Temple in Jerusalem there were fifteen ascending steps. We must deal with our relationship with God, the infinite, as we deal with life: one step at a time. Sure, you can bound up a stairway two steps at a time, but don't try it in life. Each step is a message, a lesson. An indispensable part of the chorus of experiences that shape and mold who you are—your character—and who you will become.

So it is with our spiritual lives. Our relationship with God. Multifaceted, subtle and sublime. Our inner lives too must be fashioned one step at a time.

Fifteen expressions of "praise" for God. Reaching ever higher, ever deeper. New and more stirring moments of intimacy, each one predicated on the last and each one embracing the other.

> Life is so busy, it moves so quickly. Our minds entertain a volume of thoughts in the blink of an eye. Our hearts, feelings enough to fill the oceans. And then there is our soul: longing, yearning evermore, every moment. To live.
>
> ❧   ❧   ❧
>
> You are about to enter the main body of the morning prayer service. It will open up with *Borachu*, wind its way to *Shema* and culminate with the *Amidah*, the standing prayer. As you turn from page to page and from prayer to prayer, make sure you're not alone. Take your inner self with you. Your heart, your soul, whatever it is that you feel is the ineffable you.
>
> You may want to take a moment or two now to close your eyes and calm your self. Don't be afraid. Allow yourself to feel with that other sense, that inner you, and listen with that other ear to the silent sounds. There is so much inside of us at any given moment, so far beyond comprehension, or so it seems. Now is the time to know, to whatever degree you can, who you are and to feel the pulse of your life. And now, to move onward.

Borachu / **Bless God**

Even an atheist will tell you, "If there is a God, then to relate to Him, to be close to Him, that would be the ultimate pleasure, what life is really all about."

God is infinite. And like infinity, God defies our comprehension. God, like infinity, can never be added to. He can never become more. He can receive nothing

With *Borachu* we don't "bless" God, we don't give Him anything, rather we recognize that He is the source of all existence and of all blessings. He only gives and we can only receive.

This truth is very humbling, like the relationship between master and disciple. The greater the disciple's humility—which is simply a clear recognition of reality—the greater the capacity to imbibe the craft in all its subtlety, the wisdom in all its shades. Such is the ultimate paradox. The less we know we are, the more ready we become to open ourselves and the greater we can become.

S'lach L'goy Kadosh / **Pardon This Holy Nation**

Sticks and stones will break my bones, but names will never hurt me.

Tiffany, age nine

Tiffany is right, but only if she realizes that she is also very wrong.

> *A*braham *J. Twerski, a chassidic rabbi, professor of psychiatry and the founder of the Gateway Rehabilitation Center shared this childhood recollection.*
>
> *"One of the few memories I have of being disciplined by my father for something he disapproved of was his telling me in a quiet, firm and no-nonsense tone, 'Es past nisht!' (This is not becoming of you.)*
>
> *"The message was clear. I knew what it was I was not supposed to do. However, it was only many years later that I realized the full meaning of my father's rebuke.*
>
> *"Father had told me that I was to refrain from a particular action because the behavior was beneath me. With 'Es past nisht,' father was telling me that I was just too good for such behavior. This was the furthest thing from a put-down. Instead of absorbing a message that said I was a 'bad boy,' I was being told that I was a person of excellence. The focus wasn't even on the fact that the action was wrong, but rather the message focused on me. I was above such behavior."*[11]

Labels can be either very disabling or quite ennobling. If we label our children as bad, lazy or worthless—or even if we just give them the feeling that such is our opinion of them—then we are creating a disability for them. We are making the challenge of life that much harder. On the other hand, if we label them as "precious," if we respond to their sometimes annoying questions with the words, "Yes my blessing, what would you like to know?" then we are fortifying them with emotional and psychological Wheaties.

Tiffany will be able to shield herself from all the bad names in the world if first her parents tell her what her real name is.

Pardon this holy nation, on this holy day…

In this prayer we are being labeled as holy—good, beautiful and precious—and we are being enabled. We are being told that we are eminently worthy of the opportunity to be close to God.

Shema Yisroel… Echad / **Hear O' Israel… God is One**

When a Jew dies, he dies with the *Shema* on his lips. But why? What is the meaning of this indelible bit of Jewish consciousness?

Moments before execution a prisoner is offered a final meal, a last cigarette. When we say the *Shema,* we cover our eyes and see ourselves dying—with the *Shema* on our lips.

Don't you see? It's one last chance to grab hold of what life is all about in the first place.

Create a mental list of your three greatest pleasures in life. Then ask yourself, what is the pleasure? What is the essence of that moment, that experience that caused you to feel such pleasure?

If you seek then you will surely find. It's all the same thing. *Echad,* oneness. A pristine unity. A beautiful harmony.

List your pleasures:

Friendship: Sharing, connecting, togetherness—*echad.*

Nature: To feel at one with the earth—*echad.*

Learning and understanding: To absorb and assimilate—*echad*.
Skiing: To be one with the mountain—*echad*.
Love: Closeness, to become one—*echad*.
Music: To become a part of, attuned to—*echad*.
And so on... *Echad*.

V'Haya Iym Shemoah / And If You Listen

In the second paragraph of the *Shema* we find the words, "... and you will eat and be satisfied—be careful."

Food, clothing and shelter. Once your basic needs are taken care of, then what? It seems our society has answered that question by saying "more of the same."

Food: how about Nouvelle cuisine, Cajun cooking, Mexican or thirty-two flavors of ice cream? Clothing: just take a stroll down any Mall Street USA. Shelter: an endless array of shapes and sizes with decor and appliances to match. When our society answered the question of "now what?" with "more of the same," that was a choice with far-reaching consequences, for individuals, families, society and even the planet we inhabit.

"... and you will eat and be satisfied—be careful." Now that your basic needs have been met, what are your priorities? And what do these priorities tell you about who you are and where you're headed?

> At this point in the Shema we focus on the role of *mitzvot*, commandments. Kabalistic literature defines the word "commandments" (*mitzvot*) as "bits of advice." Each commandment advises us as to what our priorities ought to be, how to stay focused and how to realize the goals embodied in those priorities.

Amidah—The Standing Prayer

Hashem Sefasai Tiftach / God Open My Lips

You've just started your own business; do you have what it takes? You've begun a program of recovery; others have done it, but can you?

Each of us is aware of our abilities and potential, and we all experience fear, doubt and hesitation. Many of our limitations in life are more perceived than real. Often, it is only phantoms that are holding us back.

---

*A*t the age of twenty-one, Bruce Seldon had already spent almost half his life in prison. Most of the crimes he committed took place in his home town of Atlantic City. In 1985 he was sentenced to ten years in jail. The prison guards found Bruce Seldon to be a difficult prisoner.

But somewhere along the way, Seldon stopped being difficult and turned his life around. He started to think about his mother who raised him..."She'll never cry for me again," Seldon remembered thinking. "I found it hard to believe this was me. I said I won't do this anymore."

Bruce Seldon stopped being a difficult prisoner, earned his high school diploma and was paroled after four years. By April 1995 he was the WBA boxing champion and ready to make his title "count for something."

He went back to Atlantic City to make amends with the owner of a liquor store he robbed, has visited Mountainview prison to speak with inmates and has spoken at almost every school in Atlantic City. And what does he have to say to the young people he speaks with?

"I tell them that dreams can come true."[12]

In Hebrew the word for lips is the same as for banks, as in river banks. The banks of a river define its limits. When we say, "God, open my lips," we are also saying, "God, help me to see beyond my perceived limitations."

Help me to see and not to be caught between the banks of fear and doubt. Help me to see the full range of my potential. Help me to see that dreams can come true.

Baruch Atah Hashem / Blessed Are You O God

The essence of all Jewish prayer and of all Jewish life is contained in the first few words of the *Amidah*. The word to focus on is *atah*, "You." We address God directly. Prayer is nothing less than personal time with God, our own private time to speak to Him. Honestly, openly and from the heart. This is the key to everything.

Va'titayn Lanu / And You Gave Us, Our God, In Love...

And You gave us, Hashem our God, in love, this day of Yom Kippur; a day of forgiveness, a day for restoring our relationship, a day for starting over again ...

It sometimes happens that parents and children drift apart. Choices are made: the choice not to write or call, the choice to ignore, to harbor a grudge, to hurt.

If Yom Kippur is anything, it is a day to restore our relationships. Firstly, with ourselves. We can drift away even from ourselves, and ultimately, all of our relationships begin with ourselves. Secondly, with the people in our lives. Mistakes have been made; oversights, carelessness, a harsh or painful word.

Restoration, return, a new beginning—new love—is what Yom Kippur is meant to foster.

And finally, with God. We often chose to avert our eyes, to pay scant attention to the gift of life, its blessings and responsibilities. We chose to cut off all contact.

"And You gave us, Hashem our God, in love, this day of Yom Kippur; a day…" To renew and to restore. To be close and to love: Ourselves, others and God.

Elokai, Ad Shelo Notzarti / My God, Before I Was Formed

God, before I was formed, did I deserve to be formed…I am like dust while I am yet alive; and surely so after my stay is completed.

Ants build anthills, beavers build dams and we build the World Trade Center. In the ultimate scheme of things, is there any real difference?

In the end, the stoic forces of nature will wash away all traces of the anthill and the civilization it housed. Little by little the dam will slowly rot or the river itself will become dry and lifeless. And what of our monuments? Are they not mere relics for the future?

We are to the universe and to time what the ant is to our planet. All but nothing, a speck of dust lost in history. With one difference: ants don't speak to God. What they say or do doesn't really matter. But our thoughts, our words and our actions do make a difference. An eternal difference.

15) I can see beyond pain and darkness and find warmth, light and beauty in the world.

16) I will not lose sight of who and what are most important to me.

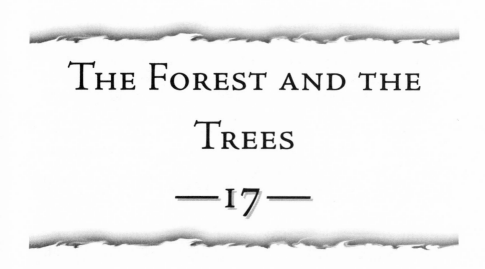

THE FOREST AND THE

TREES

—17—

Trees, Yom Kippur and Vidduy

The year was 1882 and Oscar Wilde was coming to the United States. The customs official routinely inquired if he had anything to declare. His reply: "Only my genius." Years later as he sat in prison and reflected on a squandered life, Mr. Wilde mused, "I have been a spendthrift of my genius...I forgot that every little action of the common day makes or unmakes character."

One of the most striking differences between Rosh Hashanah and Yom Kippur revolves around attention to detail. On Rosh Hashanah we grapple with life's ultimate issues: Who am I? Where do I want my life to go and what is the legacy I hope to leave? Yom Kippur, on the other hand, is a day on which attention to detail reigns supreme. Throughout the sections of the service that deal with *vidduy*—confession—(i.e., *Ashamnu* and *Al-chet*) you will find a list of sixty-seven items for which to ask forgiveness. According to the classic commentators, these sixty-seven items are in fact subject headings for even broader categories that together number many hundreds of actions for which we can ask forgiveness. It's a busy day, to say the least.

The following are two examples from the vidduy:

1) *Ashamnu* / **We Have Become Culpable:** We have acted in ways that deaden our sense of spirituality, we were driven for profit and thus transgressed God's will, we hurt others out of self-centeredness, for our own pleasure we did what we knew was wrong, etc.

2) *Al-Chet She-Chatanu Lefanecha B'emutz HaLev/* **Hardheartedness:** Refusal to admit that we can be wrong, general stubbornness, denying our shortcomings, lack of compassion for the sick and poor, unwillingness to accept advice, being tough on ourselves or others when compassion was appropriate, etc.

To say that Yom Kippur is a day for introspection and reflection is true, but it is also an oversimplification. I would like to suggest that you try a little exercise now:

Ask yourself, "How many choices have I been confronted with today?" Mind you, these must be moral choices, choices of import. Not significant life-altering choices, but those small choices that we often pass by, or through, with barely a notice. Here are some examples:

1) Did you encounter anyone today—a spouse, a child or an acquaintance—whose mood could have been lifted simply by a warm smile or a moment of genuinely expressed concern?

If yes, then ask yourself: (a) what choice did I make at that moment, and (b) how would things have been different, for better or worse, had I chosen otherwise?

2) How about your attitude in synagogue today? You can use this Yom Kippur as an opportunity for increased self-awareness and personal growth, or you can sit through another

year silently bearing the burden of a rather cumbersome experience. Have you considered that choice yet?

3) Did you have a chance to help someone today? Someone who could have managed without your help but who would have been grateful nonetheless?

Think about how long you had to make that choice. Was it more than a fleeting moment that no one but you will ever know existed?

In retrospect, how do you feel about the choice you made? Do you believe it had a lasting effect on you?

As I know you have realized, these examples are but a drop in the ocean. Everyday we are confronted with tens if not hundreds of little choices. Little, but not so little. Choices that can have either a positive or negative impact on ourselves or someone else.

There are times when we read or hear a concept, and though its meaning may be unclear, we have a sense that its profundity demands a closer look. Such a statement is the Torah's assertion that man was created "in the image of God." Its meaning is this: People, like God, have the capacity to choose. But more, that capacity defines our very essence. We are beings who choose.

This being so, it is no wonder that our days and our lives are little more than a continuous string of choices. Most of them small, some not. After all, how often do we choose a career, a spouse or whether or not to have children? These types of choices are few and far between, but there is a vast in-between, a life brimming with choices.

And thus we have Rosh Hashanah and Yom Kippur. The forest and the trees. On Rosh Hashanah we confront the major issues, the general ebb and flow of our lives. On Yom Kippur we dwell on the minutiae. Some would say that Yom Kippur is but a microcosm of Jewish life. A guilt-ridden obsession with trivialities. In fact, Yom Kippur is an affirmation of the value of life, of each day and of every aspect of each day. That which we truly cherish is that which we carefully scrutinize. The more significant the whole, the more precious are its details.

Parents are concerned about every aspect of their children's behavior. They know that how a child eats his cereal plus how he cares for his belongings, added to the way he relates to siblings and classmates, eventually adds up to the totality of that child's character. If growth and human development are not to culminate in just learning to "eat nicely," then true maturity will lie in taking the reins of the ongoing choices that shape our character.

> *The only testing ground for the heroic is the mundane. The only preparation for that one profound decision which can change a life, or even a nation, is those hundreds and thousands of half-conscious, self-defining, seemingly insignificant decisions made in private.*
>
> Senator Dan Coats

The sages in the Talmud put it this way: "A person is not given the opportunity for greatness until he is tested in the small things." Moses, the greatest leader in Jewish history, started his career as the shepherd of someone else's sheep. The same is true for King David: first a shepherd, then a king. A future Moses or a King David is entrusted with the destiny of the Jewish people only if first he is able to tend a flock with integrity and compassion and take care that the sheep don't wander off and eat a bit of grass from someone else's field.

Take care. Take care of the small, almost invisible choices. Those precious, precious details of character and life.

In the final analysis there will always exist a symbiotic tension between Rosh Hashanah and Yom Kippur. Rosh Hashanah beckons us to take a panoramic view of our lives, all the while paying scant attention to the nuance that lies therein. Yom Kippur is just the opposite—entirely nuance: the tree, the leaves, and the nourishing roots, with barely a thought to the great forest in which we stand.

Only the magnificence of the space shuttle and the unencumbered dreams out of which it grew could make man an ever-frequent visitor to space. Yet all it takes is one overlooked O-ring—a detail—to bring our dreams crashing down to earth. Or, as someone once observed, "great symphonies begin with just one note."

MORNING TORAH READING: SPIRITUALITY AS A RELATIONSHIP

—18—

A Thought about Relationships

Thanks to Hollywood's incessant teasing of our own romantic fantasies, we often develop a mental and emotional image of who will be the *right one* for me. As a result we find ourselves relating to what we hoped or imagined someone to be, as opposed to who they actually are. In such an instance we are hardly relating at all. Rather we are simply serving our own needs and desires by playing out some predetermined role, thereby ensuring a hollow, lifeless relationship.

Spirituality as a Relationship

The Yom Kippur Torah reading begins by recounting the deaths of two sons of Aharon: Nadav and Avihu. Elsewhere the Torah relates that these men died because in their unbridled desire to draw closer to God they employed an unprescribed procedure in the Temple service.

So what! So they didn't do things exactly as they were told, so they innovated a little bit; is that so terrible? Isn't it true that the only reason they deviated was because they thought this would enhance their spiritual lives and deepen their relationship with God?

Tell me if these words sound familiar:

"Frankly I consider myself to be a spiritual person... I really don't need to observe all these commandments and rituals to be a good Jew or to feel close to God. I relate to God in a way that I feel comfortable with, and I'm sure that's okay with Him."

Remember, if you relate to someone in terms of who you want them to be instead of who they are or by means that feel "right" to you but are inappropriate for them, then in truth you have no relationship at all (regardless of how good it may feel). In the dimension of spirituality, of relating to God, the same holds true.

More to Sacrifices Than Meets the Eye

During the era when the Temple stood in Jerusalem, the central focus of Jewish life was an elaborate system of communal and personal sacrifices and offerings. How is this possible? Aren't priestly orders and sacrificial rites the domain of primitive peoples bearing an elementary view of the world and how to relate to it?

Surely the Jewish people, a people endowed with insights a millennia ahead of their time, a people who repeatedly espoused ideas and values that were at odds with the prevailing mood, should have easily seen beyond these crude, barbaric practices. And what's more, how do we deal with rational, sophisticated modern Jews who to this day mourn the loss of the Temple and its sacrificial service?

Are sacrifices a disturbing historical anomaly better glossed over than scrutinized—a sort of intellectual scandal in an otherwise brilliant career—or is there some way that we can begin to make sense of that which indeed occupies perhaps a fifth of all the teachings in the Torah?

To Draw Close

In Hebrew the term for sacrifice—*korban*—literally means to draw close. The Jewish people always understood that God lacks nothing and therefore has no needs. Sacrifices are not *for* God, nor are they meant to appease Him or cajole Him to act in one way or another. The primary function of the sacrifice is to affect us in such a way as to enable us to enhance our relationship with God.

We have already pointed out that for genuine closeness to develop in a relationship you must understand and be sensitive to the one you are relating to. The flip side is that you must also possess a sufficient measure of self-awareness so that in fact it is *you*—and not some socially imposed portrait of yourself—who is involved in the relationship. And true, while we can never fully know ourselves, still, the greater our level of self-knowledge the deeper and richer will be our contribution to the relationship. The sacrifice then, in fact the entire Temple service, was a stage teeming with images that served to edify our knowledge of ourselves and how to draw closer to God.

Here are two examples from the Yom Kippur Torah reading regarding various aspects of the Temple service and how they served as educational tools to elevate our character and refine our spirits so that we could draw ever closer to the transcendental source of all existence.

1) Verses 16:7–10. "Then he shall take the two he-goats..."

Listen carefully to the detail of observance at work in this "sacrifice."

Two identical goats—identical in size, appearance and value. Both are standing in a similar manner at the threshold of the sanctuary. Both have a perfectly balanced opportunity to be used purposefully in the Temple or to be cast away and destroyed.

Is there a more poignant message for Yom Kippur? We have free will, freedom to choose our path, our actions and our destiny. We are stubborn goats, yes, but stubborn goats with a choice. Do we use our iron will to maintain our integrity and commitment to morality and God, or do we use that same will to shield ourselves from infusing our lives with a Godly dimension?

We are besieged by a host of forces, psychological and others, that lay claim to our free-willed ability to make life's most monumental choices. On Yom Kippur the eyes of the Jew are riveted on an image that proclaims our freedom. In life we must know that the power and responsibility to choose lies firmly in our hands.

2) Verse 16:14. "Then he will take from blood of the bullock... and in front of the covering he shall sprinkle seven times from the blood of his finger."

The ceremony of sprinkling the blood seven times in a downward motion also included an eighth sprinkling in an upward fashion. The world was created in seven days and thus the number seven represents the physical world and life as it is lived on a daily basis. The number eight goes one step beyond and represents that which is transcendent. This is why the *bris mila*, the covenant between man (this world) and God (transcendence), takes place on the eighth day.

I know of someone who went to India to study in an ashram for a number of years. On a return visit to Chicago he was riding a train when he became aware of something that shook him to his very core. He realized that he looked down on the people around him—ants, he thought to himself, mere unenlightened ants. He realized, "after all the lofty experiences, and after all I've learned and imbibed, if this is how I look at human beings then what have I really gained?"

The *kohen*—the priest—would first execute one sprinkle upward followed by seven downward. Our first inclinations must be directed toward that which transcends the superficial mundanity of this world. But beware. If our spiritual lives and experiences are not translated into how we live on a daily basis—in the here and now—then it is spirituality corrupted. Yes, Yom Kippur is a day imbued with lofty potential, but it is a potential that must express itself in the weeks and months that ensue.

17) I love being a Jew.
18) I will not give in to the urge to conform; I will pursue my goals and dreams.

HIGHLIGHTS OF THE MUSSAF/ADDITIONAL SERVICE

—19—

Mussaf—Additional Service

Al Chet She'chatanu L'fanechah / Because of the Grievous Error We Made before You...

The enumeration of our mistakes is a recurring theme in each of the Yom Kippur prayer services. This is because the primary opportunity of Yom Kippur is *teshuva*, return; the chance to confront and correct our mistakes.

Perhaps the most difficult mistakes to correct are those that have become habitual. Consider the following:

The Power of Habits and the Power to Overcome Habits

Nothing is stronger than habit.

Ovid, Roman poet

Habit is a cable; we weave a thread each day, and at last we cannot break it.

Horace Mann, father of the American public school

A habit is something we did for the first time that eventually became a fixed part of our character. It is hard to imagine anything more difficult than trying to break a bad habit and change a certain ingrained mode of behavior. It is particularly overwhelming when the behavior is one we were raised with from our youth or is an extension of our personality.

Jewish wisdom recognizes the powerful hold that a bad habit can have on us. At the same time it also insists that we all possess an even greater power: the power of free will.

Every person has the free will to change his tendencies. Even if a person was born with a strong tendency towards a negative trait, he has the ability to change that trait...The Almighty has given each person the ability to change by utilizing the power of initiating new habits.

Rabbi Avraham Yellin, late 19th century Eastern Europe

I disembarked at one of the most strikingly impressive examples of the Beaux Arts style of architecture in America: Union Station in Washington, D.C. I ran through the majestic and ornately restored vestibule to catch the first cab I could. After catching my breath, I engaged the imposing muscle-bound man who was driving the cab in some light conversation—the weather, sports and the meaning of life. Before long we were baring our souls as if we had known one another for years.

He told me that his father had worked on the train that ran between New York and Washington. His father's last request was that he be cremated and have his ashes spread along those tracks he had worked so faithfully. His son dutifully fulfilled that request.

"You must have been close to your father." I said. This was his reply: "We weren't close at all. You see, my father didn't know how to have a relationship with me, he didn't know what it meant to bond and to be close. I don't hold it against him though because his father didn't know how to have a relationship with him either. In our family, men just weren't close, if you know what I mean." He continued, "But I broke that cycle. It's not that way with me and my son. I made sure that we did things together, spent time with one another. I made sure we had a relationship."

The easiest thing in the world for that man would have been to *not* have a relationship with his son. He was raised in a setting that taught him that fathers and sons don't bond; he was in the habit of not relating intimately to another man. But he chose otherwise.

Of course habits and learned behaviors seem almost impossible to change. No one can underestimate the power of their hold on us. Still, there is Yom Kippur, a twenty-four hour vote of confidence in yet another power. The power to correct our mistakes and to freely choose new habits, new ways of living.

The Service of the *Kohen Gadol*—The High Priest

Tiger Woods, Bill Gates and Oprah Winfrey. Each is an icon in his or her own right. A symbol of "what makes this country great," and a model for what any kid in America can grow up to be.

You can tell a lot about a person—or a people—by those they look up to. The *Kohen Gadol* was not merely a religious functionary—he was a model of the nation's ideals. He bore the awesome burden of striving in every way to approximate the most virtuous traits of character toward which all Jews must endeavor.

V'at Zehavim / He Wore Golden Garments

The *Kohen Gadol* wore eight garments. Each garment represented a fundamental aspect of human character that the *Kohen* was reminded to be particularly attuned to.

Whenever there is an election the "test of character" issues inevitably arise. Where were you during the war? Where were you during Woodstock? Where were you when your wife wasn't looking?

For Jewish leadership, as well as for each of us, character is everything.

U'paro Mutzav / His Ox Stood ...

Life is a field to be plowed. Deeds are seeds to be planted, and the development of character is a bounty to be harvested. The ox takes one plodding step after another until finally the job is done. And so it is with us, one foot in front of the other. There is no telling how far we can go and how much we can eventually accomplish.

Achas V'Sheva / One and Seven

One sprinkling went upward while seven went down toward the ground. One sprinkle draws the eye heavenward, to the sublime. The others draw the eye to the earth, to the mundane. When the *Kohen Gadol* was immersed in the most lofty of spiritual endeavors, he always had to remain in touch with the realities of daily life.

They say you can tell the righteousness of a man by the smile on the face of his wife.

Ani U'Vaisi / I and My Family

On Yom Kippur the *Kohen Gadol* would enter the Holy of Holies (the inner sanctum of the Temple) as a representative of the entire Jewish nation. At the same time, however, the Temple service demanded that he not forget his responsibilities to his own family.

You know of course that it is easier to love humanity than to go out of your way to help your next door neighbor. A lot of people drive around with bumper stickers proclaiming "Let's Bring Peace to the World," or "Mankind: Together We Can Make a Difference." Did you ever wonder what their family lives are like?

Shigro B'Yad Ish Iti / Into the Hand of the Appointed Man

The use of the expression "appointed man" is an unusual one and also carries the connotation "the timeless man."

Fashions and fads come and go, be they clothing, diets or the latest therapy. But what about values? Are they, too, nothing but vulnerable prey for the shifting winds of societal mood?

Timeless man calls out to us; he challenges us. Raise your sights above the din of popular opinion, brave the storm and stand for something—now and forever.

The Ten Martyrs

Ayleh Ezkerah / These I Will Remember

In the words of Mark Twain, "The Egyptian, the Babylonian and the Persian rose, filled the planet with sound and splendor, then faded to dream stuff and passed away; the Greek and the Roman followed, and made a vast noise, and they are gone... All things are mortal but the Jew; all other forces pass, but he remains." And what about the French, the British and the Americans. How long until they too are relegated to the quiet halls of museum exhibitions visited only by curious strangers—and by Jews.

True, *Am Yisroel Chai*, the Jewish people live. And so do Rabbi Yishmael, Rabbi Akiva and the other martyrs. Their words have guided and inspired us for all of these centuries. But what's more, in a sense, they still speak to us. Everyday, countless students of the Talmud, of Jewish thought and wisdom, study their words in schools and *yeshivot* all over the world. Their words are alive, seriously reckoned with and hotly debated. We live because they live. But if they pass, what will become of us?

Triumph of the Spirit—A Look at the Martyrs

Rabbi Akiva

Rabbi Akiva is one of the most famous names in Jewish history. At the age of forty he was an illiterate shepherd who detested the rabbis of his day.

One day, Akiva noticed a rock that had a small, smooth hole bored through it. He soon noticed that the hole had been created by droplets of water that were dripping onto the rock. "If a drop of water can penetrate a stone," he thought, "then surely the words of Torah can penetrate my heart." This realization sparked a transformation that saw the ignorant Akiva grow into the great Rabbi Akiva, teacher of his nation.

In the end, Rabbi Akiva was tortured to death by the Romans for the crime of teaching Torah. The last words he uttered were, *Shema Yisroel...*

Rabbi Chananya ben Teradyon

Rabbi Chananya ben Teradyon was one of the preeminent sages of his day, yet more than anything he was known as a man with an overriding concern for the poor. His efforts to raise funds on their behalf are legendary.

In the end, he too became a victim of Roman savagery. Before they burned him at the stake, the Romans wrapped his body in a Torah scroll and packed tufts of water-soaked wool around his heart to delay his death and prolong the suffering.

Like Rabbi Akiva, Rabbi Chananya ben Teradyon in his final moments continued to embody the triumph of a noble soul. His final words to his disciples were, "I see the parchment burning, but the letters are flying to heaven."

Rabbi Yehudah ben Bava

Rabbi Yehudah ben Bava was fearless in his commitment to the continuity of Judaism, even in the face of the frenzied Roman drive to crush the Jewish spirit. In their attempt to vanquish the Jews, the Romans hunted down the sages of Israel and outlawed the ordination of new rabbis.

Rabbi Yehudah ben Bava ignored the threat of death that followed him everywhere. He did all he could to teach, inspire and ordain a new generation of rabbis.

Our tradition says that when he was finally caught, the Roman spears turned his body into a sieve. But the new leaders he inspired lived on, as did the Jewish people.

Ki Anu Amecha / For We Are Your People

This prayer is usually sung by the congregation together with the *chazzan* (cantor). In truth, it is a love song. Each verse expresses another facet of the relationship between God and the Jewish people.

Wherever there is depth in a relationship there is also endless nuance and subtlety, each depicting another dimension of a much greater and deeper totality.

AFTERNOON TORAH READING: THE FINE ART OF SELF-CONTROL

— 20 —

In his *magnum opus*, Maimonides codified all of Jewish life and practice into fourteen volumes. One of these volumes is entitled *The Book of Holiness*. The curious thing about this book is that it contains nothing that seems to be of a particularly holy nature. It doesn't deal with prayer, with loving God, with the observances in the Temple or anything else that one might conventionally consider to be holy.

The Book of Holiness addresses two general areas of Jewish law. One is that of forbidden foods and the other is forbidden sexual relations. So what does not eating a cheeseburger or not having incestuous relations have to do with holiness? The answer is plain. In Judaism holiness means to be the master of your physical desires. In no way do we more resemble animals than in our desire to fulfill our bodily appetites. Of one thing you can be sure: there is no such thing as an animal with self-control. Animals don't diet—ever!

Human beings have a choice. We can control our desires or they will certainly control us. The choice of self-mastery is the choice to be human. It is also the foundation of sanctity.

The Torah reading for Yom Kippur afternoon deals with the issue of controlling our most basic appetites. We can fast, we can pray—we can read the prayer book from cover to cover and pound our hearts for an entire day, but it is our ability to control and direct our desires—not to quash them—that will ultimately determine the tenor of our character.

The Haftorah of Yonah

"... and they called for a fast and they donned sackcloth, from the greatest amongst them to the smallest... and God saw their actions... and God relented."

The people of Nineveh wore sackcloth, fasted and poured their hearts out in prayer. And God responded. Not to their sackcloth, not to their fasting and prayers, but to their "actions."

God saw that their actions had changed. Isn't it obvious that this is what really counts? Our actions, our deeds, the way we live.

On Yom Kippur we deny certain pleasures to our body, to the animal aspect of our nature. We don't eat and we don't engage in sexual relations. Likewise we don't bathe, wear comfortable leather shoes or anoint ourselves with any oils, perfumes or lotions.

By taking a day off, by taking a step back from our bodily interests, we move two steps closer to the key to personal growth. When you step back from a situation you can gain a fresh perspective and regain control of that situation, of yourself and of life.

We are our actions. And we have the ability to change. Beneath it all Yom Kippur is an expression of confidence in our ability to take control of our lives.

Shepherds come in all shapes and sizes, as do sheep. Yom Kippur challenges us to either lead or follow. The choice is ours—to assert control over our own lives or to capitulate to every fragrant aroma and fanciful whim that comes our way.

NEILAH: THE CLOSING

MOMENTS

—21—

N eilah is a time of contrary emotions. Exhaustion and elation walk hand in hand. If you have tried to realize the potential for growth inherent in every moment of Yom Kippur then there is a part of you that must surely be drained. But you can't stop yet, not when the summit is so close. It's now time to draw on your second wind. This is the Super Bowl, and overtime is about to begin.

❧ ❧ ❧

In Jerusalem, everyone has a story. This story is about a lovely man named Chaim.

At the age of eighty-six, Chaim decided that it was time he began to learn a little about his religion—Judaism. He and his wife, who was eighty-five, took leave of their comfortable home in San Diego and headed, in his words, "right for the source"—Jerusalem.

These two enthusiasts spent an enchanted summer in the restored Jewish Quarter of the Old City of Jerusalem. They chose a program of study specifically designed for adults with little or no background in Jewish studies. With their arrival, the average age of the participants in this program immediately jumped by about forty-five years. The entire group adopted them as honorary grandparents.

Time passed quickly and soon these two jewels were safely back home in San Diego. Ten months later, they were back in Jerusalem.

One afternoon Chaim and I were walking together to the *Kotel*—the Western Wall. I asked him this question: "Chaim, how is it that at eighty-six you suddenly had a desire to come and study Torah in Israel? What happened?"

This is the story he told me:

I grew up in Russia and though we were proud of being Jewish, my family was not very religious. At a young age manhood was thrust upon me and I was suddenly a soldier in the Russian army.

"I knew that the holidays were approaching, but I didn't know exactly when. Rosh Hashanah came and went before I found out that Yom Kippur was only a few days off. I decided that I would fast. And you should know, this was dangerous and strictly forbidden in the army. As it was, there were days with little or no rations. Nonetheless, I had resolved to fast.

"So there I was on Yom Kippur—mile after bitterly cold mile—marching and fasting, marching and fasting, when all at once it occurred to me. If it was Yom Kippur and if I was fasting then shouldn't I also be praying? So I decided to pray. There was one problem though—I didn't know how.

"I searched my mind until I came upon the only Hebrew words I knew: Avadim hayinu l'paroh b'mitzrayim—'We were slaves to Pharaoh in Egypt.' You see, one thing my

family did observe was the Passover Seder, and for some reason those words from the haggadah stayed with me.

"These words became my Yom Kippur prayers. Avadim hayinu l'paroh b'mitzrayim—*'We were slaves to Pharaoh in Egypt.' Over and over I repeated those words. A thousand times if not more. Marching and praying, marching and praying."*

We were now standing in the shadow of the Kotel— "Somehow, somehow, I know that I am here today because of that Yom Kippur prayer."

Neilah. The starry night is closing in around us. The gates are about to close on the majestic opportunity of Yom Kippur. Chaim is our teacher now. Do you hear his message?

Somehow it's not the words of our prayers that matter, as long as you mean them, like he did. Somehow those words, that Passover passage transposed to a Yom Kippur prayer, became etched in a reality that stood by Chaim for a lifetime. Finally, at the right moment, they led him by the hand to Jerusalem.

Neilah. Just one word, one heartfelt prayer. In the end—now—that is all it will take.

I would suggest that at this time you take a few minutes to review your day. What are the one or two most important things you wanted to accomplish today? When during the day did you feel most "tuned in" to what Yom Kippur was all about; when were you most moved? At what point did you feel most in touch with yourself or closest to God? Focus on those goals and moments, those feelings and insights.

As you begin *Neilah,* ask yourself; If I could accomplish only one step of growth today, what would that step be? *Neilah* is the time to make sure that if you achieve nothing else—though you surely will—at least that one step of growth will now become a lasting part of who you are, who you will forever be.

Elokei Avraham / God of Abraham, God of Isaac

Where do I belong? Where do I fit in? Where do I even begin?

The God of Abraham, the God of Isaac, the God of Jacob. Each one had to discover who he was. As do we. Each had to become the master craftsman of his own sense of self, and with that, to fashion a novel form of relating to God.

Each possessed a singular soul and destiny. Each had a unique contribution to make to the Jewish people and to history.

It seems so very difficult. But this is what life—and Yom Kippur—is all about. Our forefathers set the pace. All we need is the courage to follow.

V'Chasmeynu B'Sefer Ha-Chaim / Seal Us in the Book of Life

Judgment is a reflection of our choices and commitments.

Have you ever assured someone with the words "consider it done." If those words mean anything, then they mean the following: "I just want you to know that with regard to the particular action we are discussing, no matter what obstacles arise, the job *will* be done. As a matter of fact, it is as good as done right now."

With determined spirits we now seal our efforts and our prayers—"consider it done."

Siym Shalom / Grant Peace . . . to All of Israel Your People

Sometimes it seems that if it weren't for the issues that divide us there would be nothing left to bind us together. What a bitter irony. Periodically, however, we are reminded of the truth that all we have is one another.

The events that made up the opening rounds of the Six Day War are legendary. But what was life like just one day before the war began?

If you don't remember, speak to those who do. All over the world Jews feared what few dared to utter, the unthinkable—

Israel would fall. A furious torrent of blood would bathe the streets of Jerusalem, Tel Aviv and Haifa.

*A*s the war began, thousands of Jews huddled together in bomb shelters all across Israel. No one knew what would be. Was this the end the Arabs had promised?

In one such shelter was Rabbi Chaim Shmulevitz. He was one of Jerusalem's great sages. A man who together with his yeshiva had escaped Europe and spent the war years in Shanghai—studying and teaching Torah to those who had escaped with him. In Jerusalem his wise counsel was sought by young and old, religious and secular.

There in the shelter together with Rabbi Shmulevitz and all the rest was a woman who seemed to be alone. Her husband had abandoned her many years before. One day he just vanished, leaving her with five young children to raise, bills to pay and no means of income. Her heart was forever shattered.

There they were deep within the earth. Would this be a shelter or would it be a grave? Her tired eyes looked heavenward.

"Ribbono shel olam, Master of the World, years ago my husband left me in a broken condition. What I have toiled to build has been a bitter fate—my life. Master of the World, I want you to know that I have forgiven that man with all my heart. I bear no grudge or hatred. Master of the World, if I can forgive him then surely you can forgive your children—the Jewish people."

At that moment, said Rabbi Chaim Shmulevitz, the safety of the Jewish nation had been guaranteed. With that prayer, the clouds of war would pass.

As Yom Kippur fades away it is time to consider another commitment: our commitment to our fellow Jews. What if we make this a year when Jews are concerned about and actively committed to one another's well-being without there being a crisis? No hostages, no terrorist attacks, no gas masks.

It's possible, you know.

Ata Notayn Yad / **You Extend a Hand**

As a wise man once said, "It ain't over till it's over."

Everyday is a lifetime. Young and vital, singing a song of the renewal of life's potential.

God's hand is outstretched. No matter where we are today, if we make a true effort to be where we know we should be tomorrow, we will succeed. The stunning power of free will is that we are not prisoners of our past. And as for our future, if you knew God would help, is there anything you couldn't do?

Elokai, N'tzor Leshoni / **God, Guard My Tongue from Evil**

Some people are highly skilled in the use of firearms. If they wanted to, they could kill. Others know how to use their bare hands, with swift and deadly motions they too can kill.

If you say the right words to a person—or more precisely, if you say the wrong words—you too can kill. This requires no special training. Likewise, the right words, said in the right way, can give a person new hope, a refreshed spirit, a new lease on life. This too we can all accomplish.

If we take our words seriously then we will take life seriously. We conclude *Neilah* and Yom Kippur as we conclude every prayer service: knowing that one word can make all the difference in the world.

19) I refuse to become discouraged; I have the ability to grow.

20) Speech is a gift; my thoughtful words can be gifts to others.

EPILOGUE:

THE MORNING AFTER

—22—

O n the day following Yom Kippur, some synagogues have a custom to begin the morning services fifteen minutes early. This custom is clearly meant to demonstrate that we have changed, that we are not prepared to step back into the same rut we were in before the holidays.

After all the efforts we made on Rosh Hashanah and Yom Kippur, our approach to life is fresh and vital. Our vigor and idealism are renewed. Our lives will be different.

A friend once offered another perspective on this custom of rising early the morning after Yom Kippur. "If you live your life differently, for even fifteen minutes," he said, "then it was all worthwhile."

The legendary Rabbi Yisroel Salanter is said to have observed that "it is easier to master the entire Talmud than to improve just one aspect of your character." To the Jewish way of thinking, life is about growth, and every step of growth is a diamond to be treasured.

If in some way this book has helped you to use Rosh Hashanah and Yom Kippur as opportunities for growth, if you have discovered a new appreciation for Jewish spirituality, for your Jewish identity, then we have achieved a lot. If you now possess an enhanced appreciation of the value inherent in Jewish life, then I would ask you, please, share this appreciation with a friend. For their benefit, for ours and for the Jewish people.

Notes

1) *The Miracle of Change:* The Path to Self-Discovery and Spiritual Growth, Dennis Wholey, Pocket Books, 1997.
2) Contemporary adaptation of a classic Hassidic tale, *The King and his Son.*
3) *Act Now*: Proven Acting Techniques You Can Use Everyday to Dramatically Improve Health, Wealth and Relationships, Dale Anderson, Ingram Price, 1995.
4) Dr. Sherwin B. Nuland, author of *How We Die* and *The Wisdom of the Body*, Knopf, 1997. From an interview with U.S. News & World Report, June 30, 1997.
5) Marty Kaplan, screenwriter, movie producer and former speechwriter for Vice President Walter Mondale. *Maybe Reason Isn't Enough*, New York Times, March 31, 1997.
6) *Extreme Sports*: Why Americans are Risking Life and Limb for the Big Rush. U.S. News & World Report, June 30, 1997.
7) *Dance of the Suffering*, from *Sparks of Glory*: Inspiring Episodes of Jewish Spiritual Resistance by Israel's Leading Chronicler of Holocaust Courage, Moshe Prager, Mesorah Publications, 1974.
8) *A Shofar in a Coffee Cauldron* from *Hassidic Tales of the Holocaust*, Yaffa Eliach, Avon Books, 1982.
9) *48 Ways to Wisdom*: Judaism's Ultimate Success Program (tape series), Rabbi Noah Weinberg, Voices From Jerusalem catalog, 1-800-VOICES3.
10) WBAL radio Interview, April 2, 1997. Brady Anderson comments on playing with broken ribs.
11) *Generation to Generation*: Personal Recollections of a Chassidic Legacy, Abraham J. Twerski, Traditional Press, 1985.
12) New York Times, September 4, 1996.

Special thanks to Rabbi Shlomo Baars for a portion of the questions in chapter five.

LEVIATHAN PRESS
BOOKS THAT MAKE A DIFFERENCE

AVAILABLE NOW

THE SURVIVAL KIT FAMILY HAGGADAH
by Shimon Apisdorf
The only Haggadah in the world…
Featuring the Matzahbrei Family. A
loveable family of matzah people that
guide you and your family through a
delightful, insightful, spiritual and fun
seder. **Featuring** the "talking
Haggadah." A revolutionary translation. Never again will you read a
paragraph in the Haggadah and say,
"Huh, what's that supposed to mean?"
Written as a companion to the *Passover
Survival Kit.*

PASSOVER SURVIVAL KIT
by Shimon Apisdorf
This internationally acclaimed bestseller,
serves as a friendly gateway through
which you will enter the world of
Passover and see it as you have never
seen it before. The Passover Survival Kit
enables you to experience one of the
centerpieces of Jewish life as insightful,
thought-provoking and relevant to issues
of personal growth and the everyday
challenges of life. This book stands on its
own and also serves as a companion
volume to *The Survival Kit Family Haggadah.*

THE DEATH OF CUPID: RECLAIMING THE
WISDOM OF LOVE, DATING, ROMANCE AND
MARRIAGE
by Nachum Braverman & Shimon Apisdorf
The Death of Cupid is divided into four
sections: The Wisdom of Marriage, The
Wisdom of Dating, The Wisdom of Sex
and The Wisdom of Romance. This book
speaks equally to singles in search of love
and couples seeking to deepen their
relationship.

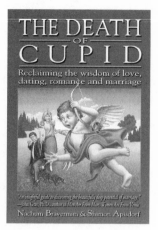

WINTER '97

CHANUKAH: EIGHT NIGHTS OF LIGHT, EIGHT GIFTS FOR THE SOUL

by Shimon Apisdorf
This book takes you way beyond the
wrapping paper to discover a little
known spiritual dimension of Chanukah.
From the lighting of the candles to the
dreidel to the Maccabees; this book
explores fascinating dimensions of this
popular holiday. Great gift, ideal for
families.

LEVIATHAN PRESS IS THRILLED TO OFFER
The music of Sam Glaser!

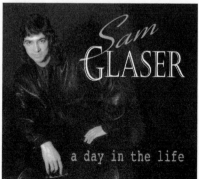

*The most rockin', inspiring
and flat-out fantastic music I've
heard in years.*
Shimon Apisdorf

A deeply inspired collection
of songs that reveal the beauty of
life through the rhythms of Jewish
living. <u>A Day In The Life</u>. **Call—**
1-800-9-SAMMYG. Mention
Leviathan Press and receive a 15% discount.

About the Author

Shimon Apisdorf is an award-winning author whose books have been read by hundreds of thousands of people all over the world. Shimon has gained a world-wide reputation for his ability to extract the essence of classical Jewish wisdom and show how it can be relevant to the essential issues facing the mind, heart and soul in today's world. His writings speak poignantly, with rare sensitivity and with humor to people of all backgrounds. Shimon grew up in Cleveland, Ohio and attended the University of Cincinnati, Telshe Yeshiva and Yeshivat Aish HaTorah in Jerusalem where he received rabbinic ordination. He currently resides with his wife and children in Baltimore. The Apisdorfs enjoy taking long walks, feeding the ducks, listening to the music of Sam Glaser and going to Orioles games. As for the Ravens: Forget it! You can reach Shimon at: ShimonA@mail.idt.net.